THE MADE-IN-INDIA MANAGER

R. Gopalakrishnan
Ranjan Banerjee

hachette
INDIA

First published in hardback in India in 2018 by Hachette India
(Registered name: Hachette Book Publishing India Pvt. Ltd)
An Hachette UK company
www.hachetteindia.com

This edition published in 2019
SRD

Hardback edition ISBN 978-93-5195-251-0
Paperback edition ISBN 978-93-88322-51-5
E-book edition ISBN 978-93-5195-252-7

Hachette Book Publishing India Pvt. Ltd
4th & 5th Floors, Corporate Centre,
Plot No. 94, Sector 44, Gurugram – 122003, India

Typeset in ITC Berkeley Oldstyle Std 11.5/17.8
by InoSoft Systems, Noida

Printed and bound in India by
Manipal Technologies Limited, Manipal

MIX
Paper from responsible sources
FSC™ C043100

THE MADE-IN-INDIA MANAGER

R. Gopalakrishnan is an author, speaker and strategist. During his professional career, he has served as Director, Tata Sons, and Vice Chairman, Hindustan Unilever. He is the author of five bestsellers: *The Case of the Bonsai Manager*, *When the Penny Drops*, *What the CEO Really Wants from You*, *Six Lenses* and *A Biography of Innovations*. He is a passionate believer that managers should write and share their learnings, for management is, after all, a performing art. He welcomes feedback at rgopal@themindworks.me.

Dr Ranjan Banerjee is Dean and Professor, Marketing, at S.P. Jain Institute of Management and Research, Mumbai. He is an internationally renowned academic, leader, speaker and writer, has been a columnist for Harvard Business Review online and has addressed numerous international academic leadership forums. He has been a contributor to leading business publications, including *Business Today*, *Business World*, *Forbes*, *Fortune* and *Business India*. A highly rated visiting professor at management schools across the world, he has also consulted with a number of corporates, such as Philips, Vodafone, Legrand, Pidilite and AXA.

Praise for *The Made-in-India Manager*

'The book presents a point of view about the evolution of Indian management thought and practice and its future trajectory. Enriched by the experience and expertise of the authors, this book provides useful insights for young managers to build on their inherent advantages and chisel career success.' – *Tribune*

'A cogently argued and lucidly written book, which can be read, with profit, by youngsters at the beginning of their careers, as well as seasoned professionals.' – *New Indian Express*

Who are made-in-India managers?

What do they do differently?

CONTENTS

INTRODUCTION

> 'India conquered and dominated China culturally for twenty centuries without ever having to send a single soldier across her borders.'
>
> – *Hu Shih*

THE WRITINGS OF THE NOBEL PRIZE NOMINEE AND CHINESE philosopher Hu Shih are very interesting – consider the quote in the epigraph taken from the speech titled 'The Indianization of China' that he delivered at Harvard University in 1937. The thought certainly is extraordinary, especially in the contemporary context of the relationship between India and China, which is today vastly different from what it was before the Second World War.

Hu Shih was not alone in admiring India's power over the rest of the world. Nobel Prize-winner Romain Rolland was a great admirer of both Rabindranath Tagore and Mahatma

Gandhi. Their ideas of tolerance, universal love and non-violence had a major global impact. Of course, they are far from the only Indian intellectuals with a global following. When Swami Vivekananda visited Chicago in 1893, the American public was mesmerized by the ideas delivered in his powerful speeches. In the 1920s, Paramahansa Yogananda's teachings on spiritualism and yoga won him thousands of followers, and decades later Maharishi Mahesh Yogi came to count the Beatles among his followers with his transcendental meditation practice.

These are all examples of India exercising influence without exercising power, a remarkable phenomenon as not many nations have influenced so many others without resorting to any military action. Harvard academic Joseph Nye termed such influence 'soft power', and India has wielded considerable soft power across the world for centuries, importing and exporting ideas and culture freely – from textiles to spirituality, dance and music, and not to mention the most important of these, yoga and food. Even in the prosaic world of management, ideas with strong roots in Indian philosophy and tradition have made a strong impression on the business world – conscious capitalism, the bottom-of-the-pyramid theory, frugal innovation, wellness and mindfulness are only a few such. This is a noteworthy and important trend, crucial to the premise of our argument in this book.

One of the central arguments of this book is that in years to come management thinking and practice could well evolve to be yet another soft power that India exerts over the world. The reasoning for this proposition is stated briefly here, though it has been developed through the book.

The Two Dimensions of Management

The skill of management, we feel, has two dimensions.

The first is the technocratic part, which answers the question: ***What is the problem that needs to be solved?*** The solution to the problem includes explicit and teachable knowledge, a hard dimension. This kind of knowledge is about concepts and techniques that are universal. Thus, terms like management by objectives (MBO), key result area (KRA), lean manufacturing and supply chain are commonly understood because they have become explicit, teachable knowledge. The development and propagation of such universal professional knowledge in management can be attributed largely to American pedagogy.

The second is the national or cultural dimension, which answers the question: ***How should the solution be executed?*** Professor Fons Trompenaars has worked a great deal in the area of culture and cross-cultural communication and their influence on management, and he posits that the application of professional knowledge is influenced by the cultural norms of individual societies. Therefore, 'promotion for performance and not seniority' is understood intellectually in the same way from Sweden to Australia, but its practice within companies varies a great deal across countries and cultures.

The management of complex organizations is an important and highly skilled task. Management is more an art than a science, and it requires positive energy to solve problems by creating alternatives and options. As Professor Trompenaars suggests, Western analytical thinking and rationality treats management as a scientific profession and functions on the premise that the positive energy required to solve objective problems is most effectively generated when the subjective context of market structure, regulations and culture takes a back seat. In societies, especially in Anglo-American ones, regulations and cultural issues tend to be less complex. In the Indian business environment, however, the positive energy of creating solutions is influenced by the drag effect of complexity, which stems from bureaucratic systems, cultural mores and assumptions, and a diversity of judgements about situations.

While managing within India, considerable energy gets

dissipated in dealing with complex cultural issues. However, in the less emotionally volatile business environments of Anglo-American nations, this positive energy is utilized much better, enabling Indian managers who work abroad to become a dynamo of managerial energy, focussed more on solving problems and less on the frictional energy loss due to basic infrastructural or systemic factors. This combined with a deep cultural inheritance of business acumen and entrepreneurship reflects in the mindset of Indian managers, a mindset by which they seize opportunities in the face of obstacles and big challenges.

This book puts forward a point of view about the evolution of Indian management thought and practice, and its future trajectory, by looking at both the past and future. We believe that the trends in Indian management practice, shaped by 'made-in-India' managers and academics, have already had an influence globally. Examining how these influences have shaped the past few decades enables us to explore how they will manifest in global management thought and practice in the future.

In order to do this, the book primarily explores four questions:

- How did management practice and the made-in-India manager evolve in India?

- What are the signs that the made-in-India manager is globally successful?
- What factors might have contributed to the success of made-in-India managers?
- How might made-in-India management thought and practice evolve in the future?

But before we begin our exploration we must define the terms that are central to our argument.

Who is a Made-in-India Manager?

In our minds, '***made-in-India managers***' are defined as those who have received their foundational education and degrees in India till the age of eighteen or a little later. They have had prolonged exposure to Indian institutions like families, communities, schools, colleges, media and politics. They have experienced the collage of strengths, contradictions and anomalies that make up India on a daily basis. After this foundational exposure, these managers may have studied or embarked on a career abroad. Over the course of their professional lives, they have most likely travelled internationally and been through a process of cultural adjustment and adaptation among international companies operating in other countries, or large local companies with practices and aspirations akin to international companies.

Consequently, the term 'made-in-India manager' does not include people of Indian origin born and raised abroad, especially during their foundational years.

In this book, we also refer to '***managers of today***' and '***managers of tomorrow***'. As a noticeable phenomenon, Indian management has really taken off only since the 1960s when two coincidences occurred. First, made-in-India managers began to have access to formal management education. Second, the educated elite started to travel abroad to study and work there in knowledge-intensive roles in science, engineering and management. We refer to managers who have had their formative education in the late 1970s and 1980s as the 'managers of today'. A new generation of managers are on the horizon, approximately those born in and around the time of liberalization, the children of liberalization. They are referred to in this book as 'managers of tomorrow'.

The Theory of Emergence

Why do we argue that management thinking and practice can be a soft power in the future? Why might it have a global impact?

We believe that a number of factors synergize in the shaping of the global, made-in-India manager. Taking each factor by itself does not make a case for the distinctiveness of the made-in-India manager. However, there occurs a combination of emergent factors that generates a new and distinctive pattern. It is to this theory of emergent factors that the arguments in this book owe their inspiration.

Emergence is central in theories of integrative systems in philosophy, botany and biology. Expressed in a simple way, a combination of simple characteristics can combine to generate a more complex characteristic that is quite distinct and different from the simple characteristics it constitutes. While some of the factors mentioned in this book, such as multiculturalism, are not distinctively Indian occurrences, other factors – such as felicity with the English language, surviving in a hyper-competitive environment and developing a high degree of adaptability – produce a combined effect that may be distinctive and produce unexpected results.

In an exploration of this nature, the influence and success of made-in-India managers and thinkers in the global scenario can also be explored in comparison with managers from other emerging markets like Brazil, Russia, China, South Africa and Indonesia. In this book, we do not compare made-in-India managers individually with made-in-China or made-in-Brazil managers because such comparison is beyond the scope of this book. It is the authors' hope that this is an area that academicians will find interesting and research further. Instead, such analysis and commentary has been made in the context of the United States (US) because the US offers a reasonable scale of immigrants, more so than many other nations. These commentaries suggest a trend in favour of the made-in-India manager.

Many Indians (and not just the few that the media write about) have seen great professional success abroad. From our experience of working with or at companies like Hindustan Unilever Ltd (HUL), we know that Indian managers are prized by their employers very highly in many cultures, including Peru, Poland and the Philippines. We have also spoken to made-in-India managers who have worked in diverse countries, including Brazil and Peru, Middle East Turkey, Thailand and Malaysia, in international companies operating in those countries or large local companies with practices and aspirations akin to international companies. Their experiences point to certain broad trends with regard to made-in-India managers that are suggestive of global success and that have the potential to influence management practice and thought in the future. Here, we must also point out that the anecdotal observations about the success of Indian managers in many cultures conceal another reality:

that, for every success we read about, there are many examples of a lack of success, if not failure. This is because the process and cultural challenges of working in cross-border and cross-cultural situations are numerous, and in any competitive situation some adjust and win, and others fail to do so. However, this does not detract from the fact that those who adapt and succeed seem to do so admirably well indeed.

Indian managers are increasingly and rapidly adapting to a global environment, and that is a good thing for the future. What we seek to do in this book is to offer a potential theory for their propensity to succeed as leaders just about anywhere in the world.

The chapters in this book have been arranged to explore this theory. The first chapters attempt to understand the influences of history, society and culture on such an individual, while later chapters are observations about young and emerging managers, their learnings, attitudes and capabilities – which are quite different from those of the managers of yesterday and today – and how these might play out in the future.

The observations in this book are based on our own experiences, anecdotes shared with us, and the personal experiences of our colleagues. Our aim was to explore the rise of the made-in-India manager through an anecdotal narration of ideas and relevant facts and data, rather than relying on scholarly research. Without doubt, data points regarding the premise of this book need further substantiation. This is not a vastly studied topic in academia or a much-debated topic in the media, but from the stories shared with us and those that we have heard about the phenomenon of the made-in-India manager, we felt this conversation is required. There are multiple views on the subject and there is no 'proven view' – and that is one of the central premises of this book as well. There is no copious, referenced bibliography at the end of this book, and most of the sources of our ideas are referenced within the text itself. We intend for this book to be highly accessible, though the underpinnings of academic literature and facts are palpable through the book.

We hope that this book provides easy, insightful reading and interesting anecdotes, that it leaves the reader with food for thought, and stirs some debate and conversation about a little-studied subject. Most importantly, we hope that reading this book will be useful for future managers to understand how the learnings from the past and harnessing their own strengths can together lead to considerable achievement for them. If tomorrow's managers succeed, then Indian management could well emerge as a future global soft power.

1 THE EVOLUTION OF THE MADE-IN-INDIA MANAGER

‘Think ever of rising higher. Let it be your only thought. Even if your object be not attained, the thought itself will have raised you.’

– *Thirukkural*

ON 1 AUGUST 2011, *TIME* MAGAZINE PUBLISHED A STORY TITLED 'India's Leading Export: CEOs' by Carla Power. Featuring Vindi Banga of Unilever and Ajay Banga of MasterCard, Powers's article asked a dramatic question: 'What on earth did the Banga brothers' mother feed them for breakfast?' The story went on to chronicle the rise of several Indian managers on the global stage, including Vikram Pandit at Citibank, Indra Nooyi at PepsiCo, Sanjay Jha at Motorola, Dean Nitin Nohria at Harvard Business School and Dean Dipak Jain at INSEAD.

In their 2011 Global Leadership Survey, the executive search firm Egon Zehnder published a study analysing the leaders of S&P 500 companies. Their study had found that Indians led more S&P 500 companies than people of any other nationality apart from American. As per the report, Jill Ader, head of CEO succession at the firm, commented that her clients wondered how it was that Indians seemed to get all the top jobs in corporates around the world.

Presenting a counter-view in an article in the *Harvard Business Review* (hbr.org, 7 March 2014), Professor Pankaj Ghemawat and Akordeon's managing director, Herman Vantrappen, examined whether CEOs were indeed India's leading export. Using mid-2013 data on Fortune 500 companies, they claimed that the number of non-Indian firms led by Indian CEOs was not very different from non-Brazilian and non-South African firms led by nationals of those countries. The two authors argued that rather than being proof of the exceptional talent of Indian-born managers, the data suggested that global companies were open-minded while choosing CEOs.

The latter view notwithstanding, there is no doubt that Indians have had much to celebrate in the success of their compatriots: Satya Nadella at Microsoft, Sundar Pichai at Google, Shantanu Narayen at Adobe, Padmasree Warrior at NIO, just to name some of the leaders of great tech companies. In academics, there was much pride when Nitin Nohria was appointed dean of Harvard Business School (HBS) and when Subra Suresh became dean of engineering at the Massachusetts Institute of Technology (MIT). As heads of international companies, Arun Sarin and Vikram Pandit, too, rose to the top of their companies, Vodafone Group PLC and Citigroup respectively.

Do India-born managers really achieve more success abroad than other immigrants? If so, why? What really sets them apart?

The late C.K. Prahalad expressed the view that, 'Growing up in India is an extraordinary preparation for management.' This statement is debatable and contentious and at the same time expresses a thought worth reflecting upon. In order to understand how the factors related to upbringing might relate to outcomes we may look outside the field of management into nature. The examples below of how this plays out are from the book by one of the authors (Gopal), *The Case of the Bonsai Manager.*

Consider this: if a baby crocodile is raised in a constricted space, its growth is stunted, and it does not grow to its full potential. The crocodile becomes 'a bonsai crocodile'. Snails are a delicacy for gourmets, and it is always a challenge to procure large and juicy snails. Left in their natural environment, snails only grow to a certain size. But when the same snails are placed in a tank with a lobster, a natural predator, they work incredibly hard to stay alive, and they grow bigger and juicier. Similarly, Japanese fishermen have found that their daily catch can be kept fresh and tasty by placing a shark in the catchment tank. The fish may have faced a challenging environment to escape the jaws of the shark, but those that escaped the shark fetched the fish farmer a very good price!

Management as a profession is largely about understanding a problem, finding multiple ways of solving it, and executing the chosen approach with colleagues and other people. The more the problems faced and overcome, the more versatile the manager becomes. A person growing up in India, whether he or she works in management or in any other field, has a large number of diverse challenges to overcome from a relatively young age. Yet, the intensity of competition to get into schools and colleges, the hassles of daily living, inadequate financial resources and infrastructure are compensated by a supportive family environment, the strong influence of values instilled by elders and an inherently spiritual bent of mind.

There are many nations in the world that have one or other condition similar to India's. Poverty and living in cramped spaces occurs in San Salvador and Egypt as well. Family values and the pursuit of a better standard of living is a recurrent theme in every society. But the combination of challenges in India is quite distinctive. Navigating those challenges while growing up endows distinctive capabilities in made-in-India managers. These unique competencies have been articulated well by Wharton professors Peter Capelli, Harbir Singh, Jitendra Singh and Michael Useem in their book titled *The India Way: How India's Top Business Leaders Are Revolutionizing Management* as: 'holistic engagement with employees; improvization and adaptability, making creative value propositions; and working with a broad mission and purpose.'

Several other views exist, attributing this phenomenon to many reasons, all of which are interesting to observe but difficult to prove. Is the rise of the made-in-India manager because of their exposure to multiculturalism in their formative years or the constantly competitive environment they grow up in? Does it hark back to the influences of colonial rule? Is it their command over the English language, or the quality of their education, or the ease with which they adapt? What instils in them the hunger to succeed? Clearly, it is a layered and complex issue.

The Evolution of Modern Indian Management

Our colonial history shows an early realization that the imparting of skills and management to locals received the attention of foreigners early on. In 1853, as the railways were just getting started in India, Karl Marx wrote in an essay titled 'The Future Results of British Rule in India', later compiled in the collected works of Marx and Engels, 'You cannot maintain a net of railways over an immense country without introducing all those industrial processes necessary to meet the current and immediate wants of railway locomotion... The railway system will therefore become in India, the forerunner of modern industry... This is the more certain as the Hindoos are allowed by British authorities themselves to possess particular aptitude for accommodating themselves to entirely new labour and acquiring the requisite knowledge of machinery... Ample proof of this fact is afforded by the capacities and expertness of the native engineers in the Calcutta mint...'

As the story of that time unfolded, and more industries and industrial activities developed in the country, we find that the erstwhile British regime realized the importance of training Indians, given the dire need for a workforce as well as the propensity of Indians to learn. The Indianization programme of Unilever, as an example, was a conscious act and began right at the time before Independence, with the recruitment of Prakash Tandon as the first covenanted officer.

In our endeavour to explore the subject we would like to argue that there are specific factors and circumstances that have influenced the post-Second World War Indian manager and shaped professionalism in India. In this context, a short history of management thought and practice in India is a good place to start.

Management as a vocation and practice has developed faster in India than in other emerging countries. India has over 4,000 management institutes – though, admittedly, only a handful of these qualify as providers of superlative management education – and every year, over 1,00,000 students gain a diploma or degree in management. Such a volume of managerial output is comparable only to the US and far exceeds that of every other country.

How and why India developed an active managerial culture compared to other developing economies makes for an interesting story. Although our first prime minister, Jawaharlal Nehru, believed that promoting business and thinking about profits should not be independent India's primary concern, the rest of the country did not necessarily follow his path. India's long-established trading traditions and their attendant values are likely responsible for this cultural perception.

A number of factors converged before and after Independence to enable a 'manager' to acquire the status of a professional in India. The railways, the Army and the civil service were all set up during the colonial era to enable the British agenda in India. As a consequence, long before Independence, these institutions gave rise to a professional workforce who were using modern work methods and living in employer-provided residential colonies where caste and religion played a subordinate role. Indians had the opportunity to perform respected and respectable public jobs, and professionalism was inculcated into them at these institutions.

During the colonial era, the British had also set up the managing agency system to achieve their mercantile goals in the jute, tea and cotton industries. A flourishing, corporate form of professional management emerged by the time India became independent. It is estimated in some studies that around 1954 there were about 4,000 managing agencies, composed of public and private limited companies, and that they managed about 5,000 companies, representing over one-fourth of the number of joint stock companies existing at that time. Being a manager was increasingly seen as an attractive option for many middle-class Indians. Unlike entrepreneurial capitalists, who thought principally of profits, money and new ventures, these professional managers were grateful for well-paying jobs and thought about how to master the techniques and tools that would help them to retain their jobs and flourish as professionals. In other words, they drew a salary to deliver a certain output of work.

After 1947, Indians were able to move into roles performed until then only by British managers. One of the authors (Gopal) narrates the story of his father, 'My father was one of the beneficiaries of this transformation. In 1931, he had come without much of an education from a village in Tamil Nadu to Calcutta in search of a job and a future. Being middle-class, he did whatever jobs were assigned to him with loyalty and diligence, all the while learning available professional skills, like accountancy. When the British managers left around 1947, he had established his credentials as a potential Chief Accountant in the insurance firm where he worked.'

In the years that followed, social factors such as population, urbanization and literacy grew in an accelerated manner and drove further change. (A point to be noted is that changes in India can be viewed as shifts in percentages or in actual numbers, and that the transformation of the country is dramatic when viewed through the latter prism. When we talk about literacy moving up from 44 per cent in 1951 to 80 per cent currently, we are really referring to 750 million additional literate human beings – a staggering figure.)

At this time, the state too had committed to the development of the public sector, and new towns came up in places such as Durgapur, Rourkela and Bhilai, following in the pioneering footsteps of private entrepreneurs Jamsetji and Dorabji Tata, who had set up Jamshedpur several years earlier.

In addition, until Independence, the established and socially acceptable professions for educated Indians were in the fields of law, the judiciary, accountancy, engineering, the civil services, the armed forces and the railways. There were degrees you could pursue to acquire the qualifications necessary to work in these fields. However, after 1947, Indian academics grappled with the problem of how to consider management as a profession in the absence of academic training. Thus, academics in the social sciences and practitioners in emerging organizations came together to develop a pedagogy to train professionals in the field. In Jamshedpur, the Xavier Labour Relations Institute (later XLRI) was set up in 1949, followed by the Indian Institute of Social Welfare in Calcutta in 1954. The Indian government started setting up the Indian Institutes of Management (IIMs) and, by the late 1950s, iconic Indian managers like Prakash Tandon, the first Indian chairman of Hindustan Lever Ltd (HLL) of the time; K.S. Basu and K.T. Chandy, also of HLL; and stalwarts of management education such as Ishwar Dayal teamed up with academics to help set up and run these management schools. When one of the authors completed his engineering studies in the mid-1960s, management was considered a somewhat risky subject to study. However, within the decade, the rise and growth of the IIMs led to a dramatic transformation of management education and professionalized it to a large extent, making it a desirable career option. So much so that leading Indian family businesses also started to realize the merits of their future generations studying management and preparing for a career in business. Families like the Mahindras, Bajajs and the Gujarati textile magnates sent their children abroad for an MBA, which additionally fostered and strengthened the professionalization of management.

Another significant initiative that contributed to the rise in status of the management profession was the setting up of professional associations for managers. Historically, most professions have been nurtured and fostered in their formative years by creating trade bodies, providing forums for training, the regular exchange of thoughts, strengthening ethics and formal teaching. Professional associations have also been an important way to promote the exchange of ideas, nurture excellence and increase the social esteem of a profession. This was the experience not only among engineers, accountants and lawyers but also among musicians, artists and dancers. However, the management profession was nascent in newly independent India. It is important to remember that even in the 1950s and 1960s, it was not widely accepted that management was something that could be taught or regarded as a profession. The setting up of the All India Management Association (AIMA) and other local management associations (the Bombay Management Association, Madras Management Association and the Calcutta Management Association were in reality precursors of the AIMA) thus gave respectability and a tremendous boost to the Indian management movement. From just one or two associations in the 1950s, there are now over fifty active local management associations in metropolitan and non-metropolitan cities. This has played a role in spreading a positive image for management education across the country, with the AIMA being viewed very favourably across the world as well.

Gaining the Competitive Edge in a Global Context

Geographically, management thought and practice were born in the cultural and social contexts of northern Europe and northern America, the early adopters of the Industrial Revolution. Much of management thought leadership and practice today emanates from a North American – we prefer the term Anglo-American – base of education and research, MBA education being barely developed in all of Europe and Japan even in the 1970s.

Here, we use the term 'Anglo-American' to signal several factors. As a subject, management education was developed by early industrialized nations like the United Kingdom (UK) and the US. Management studies and working in the Anglo-American context is more accessible for the made-in-India manager because of the Anglo-American use of English and their familiarity with it. Their advanced education and exposure to universities in the US and the UK also make the Anglo-American environment one in which they can hit the ground running. In European countries, where the language of business has lately switched to English, the made-in-India manager has only recently shown visible success with Anshu Jain at Deutsche Bank and Dinesh Paliwal at Harman International, a Samsung subsidiary.

It can be argued that talented global managers (including people of Indian origin) sometimes find it difficult to work in India. An article in the *Economic Times* by Malini Goyal (10 September 2017) lists examples of expat CEOs who do not have a record of success working in India. In many international corporations (like Unilever and Nestlé), India is perceived as a tough posting, one in which it is difficult to live in comfort and one which is hard to navigate from a work point of view. Among the positive examples that come to mind of leaders who delivered performance and also adapted to Indian ways of working are the international managers in

Unilever, like Sir David Orr (1950s), Ronnie Archer (1960s) and Joop Houtzager (1970s), who were successful during their India stints and rose to high positions globally. But there are equally many expatriates who find it difficult to give their best while working in India. Recall the situation Nestlé India's expatriate CEO faced when confronted with the Maggi noodles controversy or how a highly America-influenced Vishal Sikka had to readapt to India when he joined Infosys after he had spent virtually all his professional career outside India.

In order to understand why this may occur we have to first answer the crucial question: ***What does the performance of a manager depend on?***

As we will discuss in chapter 6, it rests on two vectors: the first is the thinking or intellectual vector; the second is the action or transactional vector. To be efficient, a manager's thinking must generate the best idea, and the resultant action must align as closely as possible with the thinking. To be effective, managers adjust the 'best idea' to be in broad harmony with the organizational culture and social mores. Efficiency is, thus, a left-brained, analytical idea, but its traction must be tempered through the social and cultural treacle in which the idea is placed, which we call effectiveness.

We believe that as management practice spread to other parts of the world from its North American origins, performance and accomplishment have always been seen to be delivered first out of effectiveness and then out of efficiency, as discussed in greater detail later in the book – the ideal being to accomplish tasks effectively and efficiently. Indian management practice, however, holds with the reality that efficiency is measured within a frame of effectiveness. The constraints to theoretical efficiency arise due to culture, assumptions and complexity.

To observe how the efficiency–effectiveness equation acquires relevance in an exploration of the creation of the successful made-in-India manager, we need to examine the particular social and cultural circumstances that breed them.

The Ingredients of a Secret Sauce

In our view, India-born managers are products of a set of four unique circumstances. Every one of these circumstances can be seen in many emerging markets, but the way they combine and synergize in India, and become an emergent factor – as explained in the introduction to this book – that sets Indian managers apart is unique in corporate and business environments across the world.

While the four circumstances are explored in detail in the following chapters, we provide here a quick overview.

Growing up in a crushingly competitive, highly aspirational environment

Because of the overwhelming importance traditionally placed on education by highly aspirational sections of Indian society, and thanks to government subsidies, higher education is a given among Indians. For example, only 2 per cent of the students who apply to the Indian Institutes of Technology (IITs) get admission in them. Getting admission into any other technology institute anywhere in the world does not pose such an intensity of competition. Yet, those who get in are not necessarily better than those who have failed to do so. Due in no small measure to the high standards of the education system in India, bright children who do not get admission into an IIT may effortlessly gain admission to Ivy League colleges in the US. N.R. Narayana Murthy famously told CBS News in 2003 that his son could not get into IIT but went on to study at Cornell, a renowned college in the US. This has positioned the IITs as genius factories, a perception promoted assiduously by IIT alumni.

Graduates from India's top institutions have also been psychologically autoclaved through high-pressure competition. They emerge as people with relentless ambition, which sometimes vastly exceeds their intellectual or financial resources. Indians are very committed to improving their status and earnings. The typical Indian has what might appear to be boundless ambition, whether he or she is an entrepreneur, manager or trader. An abundant exposure to global media and films further fans the fires of their ambition. In these ways, their aspiration soars high, though their resources struggle to keep pace. This stretch between resource and unreasonable ambition can grow to be quite significant. In fact, it was an Indian-born management researcher an academic, the late C.K. Prahalad, who articulated th gap between ambition and resource is a positive infl not just on an individual but even on a corporatior looking to develop its core competencies.

Exposure to extraordinary setbacks that accelerate pe learning

Duke Corporate Education board member Jud wrote in the *Financial Times* in 2009, 'In order develop as professionals, [students] need to b problems. A problem provides the opportu with and test one's ability to adapt.' Life for me requires enormous ability and determina adverse situations: commuting in chaotic cities, inadequate privacy and space to study at home, poor sports and library facilities and the crushing burden of exams. Almost every student has faced early setbacks: inadequate marks, a lost college admission or limited job choice. Chance, too, plays an important a role in the Indian student's life, and young people have to learn to face setbacks early on. Success is not only about being ambitious, it is also about overcoming roadblocks, sometimes through sheer persistence. Indian children learn this early on.

It should be pointed out, however, that although pressure, both from the family and peers, is high, certain social systems in India also provide the counter balance and support required to handle the accompanying stress. ortunately, parental influence and support through the dian family system is prolonged and more significant than most other societies. This helps students adapt to high-sure educational environments with relative ease. For nce, while children are often pressured into pursuing ering and medicine, their parents also tend to go the ile to ensure that they aren't distracted from their n any way and don't lack for anything as they pursue s.

The ability to work hard along with intuitive adaptability and creativity

Indians are not necessarily more industrious than people of other nationalities, but overcoming the shortcomings of (sometimes basic) infrastructure requires them to expend extra energy (that could have been more productively employed) to work around various obstacles. Educated youth across the world are encouraged to develop habits of hard work like East Asians, who derive it from their Confucian ethos. But, unlike East Asians, Indians do not have much of an aptitude for repetitive tasks. Rather, they try to complete a repetitive task differently and creatively. In short, Indians work hard and creatively – a brilliant combination.

The propensity that Indians have for hard work has been (sometimes grudgingly) acknowledged by employers the world over. Explaining how Gujarati merchants managed to capture 70 per cent of the diamond trade in Antwerp, Abraham Pinkusewitz, the head of a diamond-trading family business in Europe, commented, 'Business has always been important for the Jews but we cannot pursue it with the single-mindedness of the Indians...' (Pallavi Aiyar, *Business Standard*, 19 June 2013). Further reading on this reveals that Indians in the diamond trade are regarded as being clever, apart from being hard-working.

To put it simply, when under severe pressure, creativity and innovativeness flourish as a quick fix of a problem (referred to in India as *jugaad*). In a less pressured environment, it flourishes as sustained innovation. For instance, when the Apollo 8 mission sprang an unexpected carbon dioxide leak in the astronaut's chamber in the 1970s, the Houston Space Center did something we could consider as being very Indian – they placed all the parts of the spaceship on a table and told their engineers on the ground to come up with a solution to plug the leak using only those parts. It was a challenge to diagnose the cause of the leak, find a solution and explain to the astronauts how to execute the solution with the only resources they had at hand up. After all, in the spacecraft, they could not make a new part or alter an existing part in space. In this case, the engineers managed to arrive at a quick-fix solution, guide the astronauts on how to execute it and brought them safely back to Earth, but it is certainly a situation that required them to think around their structured practices – not an usual day in most international organizations.

Apart from the exacting demands of education and life, young Indians also have to learn several Indian languages, adapt to different school systems if their parents have transferable jobs and cope with variable teaching quality. This is quite different from, for example, the Chinese.

China as we know it today has evolved to be one of the most homogenous societies in the world with almost 70 per cent of the population being Han Chinese. They all speak Mandarin, though there are local dialects. Despite the outward similarities of geographical size and population, Chinese as a people are thus quite different from Indians.

Indian managers are often exposed to unstructured experiences that help them develop skills that allow them to flourish in any professional environment. The S P. Jain Institute of Management and Research (SPJIMR) in Mumbai, an institute that both the authors are associated with, is among the pioneers in sending its management students to dwellings of economically disadvantaged people to conduct social audits and administer practical solutions that are appropriate for them. HLL (now HUL) began the practice as early as the 1970s of compulsorily sending its elite management trainees to stay and work at rural development project sites for eight weeks. The prestigious Tata Administrative Services (TAS) programme also sends its trainee officers to participate in social and rural enhancement projects as part of the training. Such practices have spread among companies and elite government officers, and, as observed by the authors, the scale is unprecedented in other societies.

India is rapidly becoming multi-cultural as communities migrate, inter-marry and learn about cultures across regions. Although the phenomenon of inter-caste or inter-linguistic group marriages has been recent, its urban proliferation brings challenges of adaptation that many other societies cannot comprehend. In Chetan Bhagat's novel *Two States*, and the film that was made from the novel, this was brought out lucidly and amusingly.

The ability to think in English

The global language of business is English, and language proficiency plays an important role in both success and socialization. Since the adoption of Macaulay's Minute, Indians have learned and spoken the English language fluently. In fact, many upwardly mobile Indians from diverse communities and smaller cities and villages place a great premium on learning English. Families with modest incomes would spurn free municipal and government education and pay for English-language education even if it was expensive for their income level. In many small towns of India, one can see English-speaking language skill development schools, something we would not encounter in South American or Chinese small towns. Professional education for most Indian managers is almost certainly in English, and the case studies they read are Anglo-American.

These circumstances come together in various combinations to produce a sufficient number of highly competitive, creative and competent potential managers. Made-in-India managers are, thus, not only culturally and socially trained to be effective in Indian conditions, which are highly variable and kaleidoscopic, but can hit the ground running in any overseas employment. Far more instinctively than their counterparts elsewhere, made-in-India managers assess a professional landscape, the soft factors around an issue, and act in a manner in which they rock the boat without any risk of sinking it. The trade-off between efficiency and efficacy is quite intuitively made by them.

When made-in-India managers follow their thinking vector, they make brilliant analyses and articulate solutions impressively. When it comes to implementing the action vector, they cross the river by feeling the stones. An interesting phenomenon has been observed in this regard. Economists and politicians typify the expression 'cross the river by feeling the stones'. While they show a high level of thinking when commenting on how things in the country can improve, and their vastly different views tend to aggregate around certain themes, when it comes to implementation the dissonance between the thinking and the action vectors are very stark. For instance, removing a fertilizer or cooking gas subsidy is an easy announcement but in reality it requires exceptional care because there are many points of view to be considered because of the complexity of Indian demography.

When it comes to India-born managers, a similar dissonance arises. It has been seen that while working abroad Indian managers adapt to policies like flat organizational structures and promotion by performance. However, when they are in India, they revert to the traditional penchant for designations and anticipation of promotions that are expected to take age and seniority into account. As an instance of this, HUL, as an organization which has many managers in India and India-born managers stationed abroad, was stymied by the differences between their attitudes to work and work relationships within India and abroad. Another example came to the fore when India Inc. went on a mergers-and-acquisitions spree in the mid-2000s. A new and strange phenomenon occurred: managers in companies that had been acquired were used to being told by the new owners what the way of working would be. That is standard international practice. But companies like Novelis, Corus and Brunner Mond were bewildered when their new owners chose not to impose the parent culture and will on the acquired companies. The new owner wanted to adapt to the acquired company rather than the other way around.

It becomes evident, then, that when made-in-India managers work in Anglo-American environments, the dissonance between the thinking vector and action vector is reduced. Being analytical thinkers and generally highly engaged employees, they implement ideas and solutions with commitment, sensitivity and efficiency. It is no wonder that their contribution is noticed and applauded within their organizations.

■

In order to bring together all that has been said so far, let us take a look at the first made-in-India managers and academics who blazed a trail into the West.

The earliest rise of the professional Indian manager was the appointment of made-in-India CEOs to head the subsidiaries of multinational corporations in India. In 1959, J.M. Lall was the first Indian to be appointed chief executive of ICI UK. Soon after, in 1961, Unilever appointed Prakash Tandon chairman of HLL. Imperial Tobacco UK appointed Ajit Haksar chairman of ITC India in 1969. These events in the 1950s and 1960s set in motion the 'Indianization' of the management leadership of Indian subsidiaries of multinational corporations (MNCs), and gave greater visibility to made-in-India business leaders.

Following this phase, made-in-India managers started to get appointed to top-level positions in parent companies. T. Thomas, chairman of HLL, joined the Unilever board in 1979. Almost without a break since then, the Unilever board has included at least one made-in-India leader. P.K. Nanda, CEO of Metal Box India, was elected to the parent board of Metal Box PLC at about the same time.

Since those early appointments, many others have followed. Made-in-India managers were also being appointed CEOs of global companies. Rajat Gupta was appointed managing director of McKinsey and Company in 1994. Indra Nooyi became global CEO of PepsiCo in 2006. She was followed by Ajay Banga at MasterCard, Vikram Pandit at Citigroup and Rakesh Kapoor at Reckitt Benckiser. More recently, the technology industry in California has seen the rise of made-in-India CEOs like Satya Nadella at Microsoft, Shantanu Narayen at Adobe and Sundar Pichai at Google. The venture capital and financial services businesses too have produced their share of significant successes like Vinod Khosla at Sun Microsystems, Kavitark Ram Shriram and Berkshire Hathaway's Ajit Jain.

Moving to the academics, in the emerging markets, as we have already discussed, India was perhaps the first to begin teaching management as a subject. The growing importance of the IIMs, the more than 1,00,000 management graduates from over 4,000 management institutions, the vibrant AIMA all point to an early flowering of the management movement, long before Europe and second only to the USA.

Professor Ram Charan was most likely the first made-in-India academic to have achieved a Harvard doctorate in 1967 and was offered tenured professorship there. A very talented cohort group of made-in-India management academics has been spawned over the last several decades – the late Professor C.K. Prahalad, the late Professor Sumantra Ghoshal, Professor Dipak Jain, Professor Nitin Nohria, Professor Krishna Palepu and Professor Vijay Govindarajan are only a few of the names that light up this universe of stars.

This constantly growing list of accomplished and talented Indian-born managers and academics only bolsters our point of view that there is some secret sauce that goes into the making of the India-born manager. The recipe of the secret sauce remains to be explored in its entirety, but its existence is not in doubt as the many examples and comparisons in this book suggest. Here, we attempt to analyse the ingredients and put forth a point of view about how they are synthesized into creating that secret sauce.

2 THE TRADING GENE

'Continuity rather than change was the hallmark of Indian business until the nineteenth century… The structure remained family-centric…and professions were caste based.'

– Professor Dwijendra Tripathi,
(ex-faculty, IIM Ahmedabad)

MANAGEMENT WAS THE CHILD OF INDUSTRIALIZATION, WHICH created large firms. Industrialization was the child of trading, which created far-flung markets for local produce. Thus, we believe, trading is the ancestor of both industrialization and modern business.

Many societies with a history of trading and entrepreneurship developed robust systems to support such enterprise. For instance, the Roman Empire of the early centuries developed a sophisticated economy and established a coinage system. The Medicis of Italy developed a fine banking system. Some historians count the Roman Empire that flourished at the beginning of the Christian era, the Chinese Song dynasty at the end of the first millennium, and the Mughal empire in India in the middle of the second millennium as some of the most powerful trading nations before the Industrial Revolution began. It is indeed fair to say that trading is the starting point for business. It gave birth to the practice of management systems; the businessmen and traders of our past are the 'professional' ancestors of the managers of today.

We do not seek to place the Indian trading and entrepreneurial inheritance on a pedestal. Our attempt is merely to enumerate the systems and strategies as they have been practised through the ages and reverse engineer them to explicate the link between ancient Indian trading practices and modern management principles.

The Inheritance of Principles and Attitudes

The Indian trading tradition developed 1,500 years before the Mughal empire, and it is among the oldest systems in the world. Dating back to the pre-Christian era, India's trading systems and practices became advanced quite early on. Trade in pre-modern times included commodities as well as manufactured goods, principally textiles.

These days, people choose business as their career, but traditionally trade chose only those committed enough in a family to join the business. The modern-day equivalent is that the top MBA colleges choose a minuscule number of students from the thousands who apply for a management education. Over the last 50 years, of the estimated three million Indians who have acquired a formal management education, many are modern versions of the traditional trader. They have new names like investment banker, private equity investor, hedge fund trader, FMCG marketer and software professional, but in essence all of them are buying something at a cost, adding value, selling the product at a higher price and making a legitimate profit, all the while overcoming competition. This sequence of activities has been going on for centuries.

Indian business, management and entrepreneurship traditions suggest that striving for well-being and material gain (*artha*) was a positive goal that every human being must aspire to. The *Arthashastra*, the world's first economic treastise, is, in many ways, a manual on the rules of business policies; for example, the text laid down that the trader should make a profit, but a legitimate profit; that wealth creation is subordinate to ethics and morality; that 'business' and 'profit' are not dirty words.

It has always been the duty of the trader and businessman to buy, sell and make a profit – just as it was the duty of the Kshatriya to defend the country and the ruler to administer righteousness (dharma). The *Arthashastra*, then, is, in some ways, India's first corporate legislation – the Companies Act, 300 BCE, if you will.

It is worth exploring further the inherited traditions from the *Arthashastra* and its explanations that in some ways continue to influence the Indian business context.

Attitude Towards Religion

In the author's experience, business and religion are far more closely connected in India than anywhere else in the world. In Western societies, even if there were traces earlier, the Enlightenment period of history separated most business from the rituals of religion. In many Asian economies, business and trade as practised today are not at all connected with rituals of religion, even in the Arab world. But India is different.

For centuries, the Indian trader has regarded *vyapar* (trade) as his religion, the shop as his temple and profit as the fruit for his hard work. Observing a modern *vahi* puja during Diwali, whether at small shops or large corporations, shows us the fervent rituals of treating business as religion and profits as fruit. One can also experience the intertwining of business and religion at the puja for the inauguration of a new factory by a modern company. Such events are replete with chanting of prayers, offerings of flowers, breaking of coconuts and vermillion markings on the forehead. Such an intimate connection between the two has not been witnessed anywhere else in the world.

There have been several well-documented cases of famous businessmen and business leaders who are known for their deep religiosity. In India, marketing and sales decisions are also intrinsically linked to religion. For example, a relatively unknown auspicious day, Akshaya Trithiya, has now become one of the most important days in the year for the sale of gold and ornaments.

The Importance and Role of Dharma and *Artha*

These days, the words 'politics', 'government' and 'business' carry a negative association with corruption. The malaise of corruption is ancient in origin, and societies everywhere will continue to fight it for centuries to come. Among strong trading communities like India's, being a trader comes with high status, though the overall image of the businessman in Indian society has been reported to be unflattering in recent years.

When Jawaharlal Nehru expressed his view that 'profit is a dirty word' to industrialist J.R.D. Tata, he was perhaps reflecting his Western influences – his education abroad and exposure to the ideas of the Fabian Society. He could also have been reflecting the words of the *Arthashastra*, 'merchants are all thieves, in effect, if not in name.' The *Arthashastra* also states, 'Just as it is impossible to know when the fish swimming in water is drinking water, so it is impossible to know when government servants in charge of undertakings misappropriate money.'

Despite these assertions, the foundation of business in India was built on the premise of earning legitimate money, which is deeply tied into the ideal of living a life of dharma. A business person is thought by the Hindus, Buddhists and Jains to be born into debt because he inherits endowments from his ancestors. He is expected to repay his debts to his ancestors, God and society through the course of his life by giving back to society. His life is thus part of a karmic circle.

While a trader must earn a profit, the *Arthashastra* places lesser importance on profit-making than on morality. The hierarchy specified is dharma, *artha*, *kama* and moksha – morality, profit, pleasure and redemption.

How did this tradition play out in the past and how does it manifest in modern times?

Dharma was about doing the right thing, whether in private or public life. Traditional texts state that commerce is the religious duty of merchants. A business must make profits, but it must be tempered with righteousness. The Atharva Veda states rather ambiguously that the conduct of righteous people is dharma. So, dharma is the practice emanating from good people, it is the moral act and also the reward for doing the right thing. This is a deeply ingrained philosophy in the Indian business context. For example, when Vijay Mallya did not pay his workers, it was not just a breach of an employment contract (as in the Western tradition), but an impairment of livelihood as the Indian tradition suggests. It is no surprise that Mallya was pilloried by the media and public opinion because he had breached dharma while protecting his own *artha*.

The emerging laws of corporate governance in India are modelled on Anglo-American experiences but their implementation is not rooted in an Indian ethos. This constantly throws up contradictions and anomalies. For example, a board has the right to fire a CEO as per Anglo-American as well as Indian laws, but the debate on the dharma of firing the CEO is a long-drawn-out and excruciating one. In India, how a company parts with a CEO matters just as much as whether it exercised its legal right in a proper way. Indian firms tend to let a senior person resign 'quietly' rather than be perceived to have sacked him or her.

Another example is the role of independent directors. Culturally, we would like them to act as mentors and wise elders. The laws of corporate governance require the independent director to be an activist and interventionist. These opposing demands on independent directors produces piquant situations. There have been instances when an independent director has acted in an interventionist manner, causing the majority shareholder to express displeasure in some form. If the independent director has failed to intervene, then the director is pilloried for sleeping at the wheel if and when something goes wrong. This is illustrated by recent events related to corporate governance at Kingfisher Airlines, ICICI Bank and IL&FS.

In 2009, the board of directors of Axis Bank voted 8:1 in favour of appointing an outsider, Shikha Sharma, as CEO. At the time Sharma headed ICICI Prudential Life Insurance. The dissenting vote was that of the chairman outgoing CEO, P.J. Nayak, who favoured an insider for reasons which he placed before the board. His view was against the wishes of the government, which was the majority shareholder of the bank. It is a matter of record that differences had started brewing between the chairman and the finance ministry and regulators long before the voting event.

Engagement with Trade and Business

Trade engenders a level of engagement among Indian traders that is all-consuming and all-pervading. After all, trade is their source of livelihood and has significant connotations of status and commitment. It is somewhat similar for the traditional trader's successor, the Indian professional manager. While their jobs consume only 35 to 40 per cent of a 24-hour day, the outcomes of their jobs take up 100 per cent of the managers' emotional capacity as well as their family's.

To Indian managers, job accomplishments and career progression matter so greatly that they define who they become, how society regards them and what they stand for. As a result, Indian managers are hugely engaged with their organizations, and are deeply involved with both the work and the relationships that their jobs entail. It has been widely seen that many Indian executives fail to develop a hobby or any other interest and display signs of crumbling after retirement, their jobs having been the be-all and end-all of their lives.

Risk-taking and Reaching Out

It is the task and duty of the trader to take sensible risks and welcome uncertainty. Western risk management techniques are centred around mitigating risk and reducing turbulence. Indian risk mitigation involves dealing with the upheavals, and not necessarily judging if the situation and its oucome is good or bad. This seems to have become the way to deal with trouble and uncertainty.

We do not suggest that the Indian trader is unique, but we do claim that the information asymmetry of the Indian trader is higher. Hence, trade is more volatile in India. The Indian trader believes that the opportunity for profit is born in unpredictability. Excessive trading stability is not conducive to profit-making, and the trader is trained to gain from the uncertainty of business trading. For example, price information of commodities in other markets is crucial to a trader's way of doing business. When Bombay was a major cotton trading centre in the late 1800s, information on cotton prices in other markets needed to be obtained a bit earlier than other traders to reap a competitive advantage. Premchand Roychand, a shrewd trader of the time, used small boats to go out into the Arabian Sea to exchange information with ships that were waiting to enter the harbour. In this way, he leveraged the uncertainty of market knowledge to obtain valuable information that would enable him to trade smarter. Today, of course, traders do this all over the world through the Internet.

This longstanding tradition ties into the current obsession with the Volatile Uncertain Complex Ambiguous (VUCA) world. Traditional Indian practices among the trading community advanced the skill of leveraging the VUCA factors rather than suppressing volatility or wishing it away. The importance of these factors is best understood through the personal experiences of today's made-in-India managers who have worked through ambiguities in their growing years in the Indian environment. These experiences are considered by those managers to have improved their innate skills at coping with unpredictability and helped them to succeed at a global level.

The Development of Managerial Skills

The history of the traditions and systems in various trading communities of India show the inculcation of early trading skills: adaptiveness to other cultures, learning by doing, following financial rules and systems, and providing support systems to compatriots. In general, the environment in which children grow up in India presents challenges, including turbulence and intense competitiveness, which hone their problem-solving abilities. The examples given here are modern and may not appear as hard-driving as the experiences of yore. They are meant to demonstrate how the vast range of crucibles of experience in India can make Indian managers tougher and hungrier than their counterparts in other parts of the world.

Prasenjit Basu, a distinguished economist in Singapore, is a product of St Paul's in Darjeeling, St Stephen's in Delhi and the University of Pennsylvania. He has spent a quarter of a century analysing Asia's economies for his clients. While speaking of the influences to which he attributes his success he mentions his early experiences in mountaineering, getting ragged at college, and negotiating with labour at a tea plantation in North Bengal. Circumstances had him staring at a complete loss of self-confidence, and then forced him to learn how to negotiate from a position of strength, he says.

K.V. Rao, Tata Sons's resident director in Singapore, grew up in Pondicherry in an Anglo-French environment. With a sacerdotal family background, going into trade was nowhere on his radar. However, his irrepressible urge to study was encouraged by his family and, through a series of intriguing twists and turns, he acquired a degree from the Indian Institute of Foreign Trade, Delhi. His real learning, as he describes it, came out of the *shagirdi* (mentorship) of some of his early bosses. Such relationships, he holds, produce conversations that impart lessons for your life and career. He makes special mention of the career advice that he received – about being a good performer, diligently adhering to his principles and waiting for the rewards of his hard work.

Accomplished academic Phanish Puranam, now at INSEAD Singapore, first trained in music. Not surprisingly, he uses the *gharana* metaphor to explain that like the connect between a *guru* and a *shishya* among Indians the relationship between a junior and senior colleague is much deeper than simply the imparting of skills or education. He goes on to say that his research associates have a far more engaged relationship with him as compared to other professors, though some may like it and some may not.

Dinesh Paliwal, CEO of audio and technology major, Harman International, has lived and worked in six countries. He gives much credit, to America for being a meritocracy par excellence. However, he concedes that 'competing daily to even walk around in a 1.3 billion population' does create distinct characteristics in Indians like understanding real consumer needs and redesigning business models, much like what Nirma did with their low-cost detergent, and Velvette with the shampoo sachet.

The 7S Framework of Traditional Indian Practices

While we recognize the inheritance of an exceptionally strong trading tradition in the Indian businessman and management professional and understand that this tradition was encoded into practice we can equally reverse engineer historical records to further cement the linkage between trade and management.

Modern management has evolved with words and concepts like 'framework', 'systems', 'processes' and 'role definitions'. In management jargon, organized work is specified through systems and processes. These systems and processes fit into a framework of structures and roles. By reviewing the business traditions of the past, one may be able to piece together how today's made-in-India manager's strategic thinking functions in the areas of entrepreneurship and management. We have tried here to reconstruct observations and evidences into a possible design, but using modern ideas and terminologies.

In the 1980s, McKinsey garnered considerable acclaim for presenting the 7S framework for business success. The 7S model is an enlightened, analytical framework born in the crucible of Western thought leadership. Traditional Indian trading practices have been sketchily recorded, but many of them continue to be practised to this day. Assembling the facts available, we can analyse whether Indian business practised something like the 7S framework without being aware of the analytical technique. A lot of the information mentioned here has been extrapolated from the scholarly series of almost ten books in the Story of Indian Business series, edited by Gurcharan Das.

The 7S framework of mangement, which holds that there are seven internal aspects of a company that must work in tandem for the assured success of an organization. Of the seven, the three hard elements are:

STRATEGY

STRUCTURE

SYSTEMS

The four soft elements are:

SHARED VALUES

SKILLS

STYLE

STAFF

The points made below are illustrative rather than definitive, and historical evidence has been retrofitted to the modern 7S model.

Strategy

Trade was built on specific competitive advantages – trust, domain knowledge, supply chain and information.

Trust was an important competitive platform. Merchants were prominent members of society in Tamilakam (ancient Tamil country) and were held in high esteem. The merchants of Poompuhar on the eastern coast (near modern-day Nagapattinam) were described in literature as being 'as straightforward as the crosspiece of a yoke...they value their goods and goods of others by the same standard... they openly state their profits...' (*The Merchants of Tamilakam*, Kanakalatha Mukund, 2012). In the famous Sangam epic *Silappadikaram*, the central characters of the story belonged to one such eminent merchant family from Poompuhar.

The Tamilakam traders also had great domain knowledge, and were skilled and knowledgeable about assessing the commodities they dealt in. Based on the commodity, they organized themselves into guilds as corroborated by the geographic distribution of inscriptions.

Supply chain management was yet another competitive advantage. The Kutchis from Gujarat acquired a deep understanding of ship-building and navigational techniques. They were able to leverage wind patterns, ocean currents and the stars above more skilfully than any other Indian trading community. These abilities enabled them to trade with Oman, Zanzibar and East Africa.

Information, both explicit and implicit, was the final competitive advantage. Mandvi on the Gujarat coast became a market city, somewhat like what Dubai has become in modern times, and was teeming with Arab and African traders apart from the local Kutchis. The Mandvi merchants possessed information on every local market, whether in India, Oman or Zanzibar, and their market expertise enabled them to succeed in every market.

Structure

On the western coast of India, just north of modern-day Kochi, there used to be a thriving port called Muziris. A papyrus scroll in the Vienna Museum dating to around 100 CE has a contract written in Greek between two merchants, one in Muziris and another in Alexandria. There are other evidences of written contracts, covering the duration of the voyage, the quantities and value of the goods traded and, finally, the payment terms.

Multan, in the north-western part of the country, was a thriving trade centre. Here, traders from different countries in Central Asia and Persia came to trade with Indians. The Multani Indians were perceived to be particularly successful. They mastered the technical skills to conduct long-distance trade relations and designed a fully integrated commercial structure comprised of local agents and dispute resolution representatives all over north India. The family-run firm was at the heart of their system, but to run a far-flung business, they developed systems of senior and ordinary agents all over their territories of interest.

Systems

As discussed earlier, Poompuhar was a major trading port of Tamilakam. From the description of the city in *Silappadikaram*, it appears that seven commodities (cloth, gold, grains, salt, oil, ploughs and jaggery) were regularly traded, and each had its own guild. City streets were designated according to the commodities, and shops were quite specialized. Flags were used to signal the location of the shop and the goods traded in that shop. There were numerous toddy shops for weary travellers to unwind at and as per one account, 'the flags for toddy shops were so numerous that sunlight could not penetrate onto the street below.'

Among the caravan traders of Multan, evidence shows that a *hundi*, a bill of exchange drawn up in a formulaic language, was used. An English trader called Burnes wrote about how he '...could use my Indian *hundi* in Nizhny Novgorod, Astrakhan and Bukhara.' Multani traders had a hierarchy of a general market broker (*dalal*), grain market broker (*baqal*), agents (*gumastha*) and moneylenders (*saraf*). These were fairly sophisticated commercial systems for the times.

Shared Values, Skills, Style and Staff

American political scientist Francis Fukuyama has explained how India exhibits traits of a weak state–strong society, while China exhibits traits of a strong state–weak society. India has held together as a state through the village, caste and family rather than through central political power (as is the case with China). For good or bad, this is still evident in modern Indian politics as well as in social policies and practices. Evolving trading practices also relied on this hierarchy of village, caste and family and, arguably, this has been carried into modern corporations as well.

Max Weber had cited the Protestant ethic (thrift, hard work and rationality) as the reason for the adoption of the Industrial Revolution and the accumulation of financial resources by northern Europeans and Americans. The history of Indian entrepreneurship suggests that a risk-taking pursuit of *artha*, subordinate to the higher goal of dharma, can also work for economic advancement. The Marwari ability to adapt to situations and their flexibility of mind are important factors in their extraordinary success. The Marwari concept of the *basa* was originally to provide a cooperative lodging for fellow migrants from Rajasthan. However, these *basas* evolved into informal training schools and networks for like-minded businessmen. The Marwaris have also used their connections for business through *gumasthas* (agents) in distant areas.

For the Multani firm, the family was at the centre, and at the heart of the family was their reputation. Without a good reputation, it would be impossible for the firm to thrive in business. Shared values in this area were essential for the survival of the firm. Over many years, apprentices were trained in critical areas like accounting, the use and rules of *hundis*, the procedures to determine interest rates and the legal systems to sort out differences. To use the language of the modern MBA, apprentices were trained in business finance, pricing and business law. This training was considered by the Multani traders to be critical to the firm's success (human resources).

The management development and succession planning system of the Chettiars of Tamil Nadu is also a very interesting and intricate one. When a boy in a family turned eleven years old, he was inducted into the business as a trainee (*podiyan*). He worked for a decade as a *podiyan* and then became an assistant (*aduthavan*) for another ten years. In the third decade of his career, he became a shareholder (*pangali*), and at age forty-one he was groomed to be chief (*muthalali*). This system is brilliant and can stand alongside any modern management development system.

Trade and entrepreneurship have flourished in specific communities, usually along the coasts of the country. Attitudes, practices, systems, shared values and culture have evolved in myriad ways, and these have been captured within business families. There is, therefore, an evolutionary nexus between trading, business and management.

While we have laid out the influence of a legacy of trade and commerce on the made-in-India manager, we need to examine the larger societal and cultural influences that equally come to bear on the made-in-India manager. This is explored in the next chapter.

3 THE CULTURAL LEGACIES OF A COLLOIDAL SOCIETY

'A nation's culture resides in the hearts and souls of its people.'

– Mahatma Gandhi

'Cultural analysis sees the tapestry as a whole, the picture and the weaving process, before attending to the individual threads.'

– Mary Douglas

A SOCIETY RELEARNS ITS PAST AFTER EACH NEW ARCHAEOLOGICAL discovery. Until that point, the people of that society do not know exactly what their past is, but that does not mean that they did not have a past or that the past has had no influence on them. Consider the discovery of the 4,000-year-old Indus Valley civilization through the excavations at Mohenjo Daro between 1919 and 1926. Contemplate the richness of Tamil as the world's oldest language, evidenced by the inscriptions and poetry of the Sangam era. They bear testimony that the past does and did exist, though we may only discover it one item at a time.

The study of history and culture enables academics to explore the evolution of human characteristics and habits. Using the results of such studies insights and hypotheses can be offered to explain what we observe today. The emergence of the modern, recognizable made-in-India management practitioner and thought leader on the global scene has been shaped over the last five decades, though the inheritance and tradition of business management is much older. What, then, about India and Indian society allows for such a diverse set of factors to thrive and influence the business sphere? The answer, we think, lies in the kind of society India is and the environment that it engenders.

Colloidal India

In 1956, in *Colonial Policy and Practice*, the economist J.S. Furnivall wrote about a 'plural society' as one in which there exists a medley of peoples, a medley in which the constituent people mix, but do not combine. 'Each group holds its own religion, its own culture and language, its own ideas and ways.' This was a plural society with different parts of the community living together yet separately. We could also call such a society a colloidal society.

To understand what a colloid is, we must recall our school chemistry lessons. There are three types of mixtures. If you add sugar to water, the mixture is called a solution because the sugar dissolves in the water. If you add uncooked rice to water, it settles at the bottom as a precipitate. If you add wheat flour to water, it disperses into the water. This dispersed mixture is called a colloid because the wheat flour neither becomes a solution nor settles at the bottom, it disperses and stays dispersed.

If you shine a beam of white light into a transparent glass full of the colloidal mixture of wheat flour and water, the white light does not pass through. It reflects back as blue light due to an effect called scattering. In science, the attribute of a colloid reflecting light in a completely different way is called the Tyndall Effect.

What does this have to do with India or Indians? Indians are perhaps the only colloidal society in the world. Multiple religions, ethnicities, languages and castes and many other diversities stay suspended in the cultural milieu of Indian society. Any light that you shine on India scatters back in different hues in a sort of Tyndall Effect. Contrast this with Chinese society, which is homogenous and 92 per cent Han! The point is not which is better – the point is to accept who we are, and then to leverage our strengths as we move ahead.

The following are some of the more interesting factors that contribute to India's colloidal nature.

Longevity of Civilization

In 1905, Allama Iqbal, an Urdu poet in undivided India, wrote about his country:

Yunan-o-Misr-o-Ruma, sab mit gaye jahaan se,
Ab tak magar hai baaqi naam-o-nishaani hamarà.

(Greek, Pharaonic and Roman civilizations have all vanished,
But our civilization survives and thrives).

These lines are predicated on an important fact. Our origins lie in an ancient civilization and a number of our cultural practices derive from this well of antiquity. For instance, even today, the Vedic rites observed in Hindu marriages, the rituals in temples, and the practices at religious places like Mathura and Varanasi demonstrate how unchanged some traditions still are.

India has conserved tradition while constantly adapting to new influences with some benefits (keeping alive so many spoken languages) and some penalties (promoting rituals and prayers, emphasizing societal hierarchies to maintain order amidst rapid change). Whether these traditional influences are considered advantageous or disadvantageous depends on the individual perspective, but they are very real in the Indian context.

Such a long-lived civilization also passes down characteristics to the next generations in some not-so-clear ways. Academics who study the evolution of people and societies do so by tracing the history of language, music, trade practices, genetics and soft power over other societies. The evidence of the influences of tradition on a community's lifestyle, language, culture and mindset makes it interesting to imagine their effect on management organization, thought and practice.

Diversity in Religion

India is home to all the Abrahamic religions. The Jews first came to the coast of Kerala approximately 500 years before the birth of Christ and after that migrated to India over the years, driven by trade or persecution in other lands. The Jewish people have lived in India as a separate community following their own customs and mores and yet have harmoniously integrated into Indian society. When the Pakistani Lieutenant General A.K. Niazi signed the documents of surrender after the liberation of Bangladesh in 1971, Major General J.F.R. Jacob, an Indian Baghdadi Jew, played a key behind-the-scenes role in accomplishing this result. Maj. Gen. Jacob always maintained that he was first an Indian and then a Jew.

Christianity arrived in India in the first century CE, long before it entered Europe when the apostle of Jesus, St Thomas, landed in Kerala. Likewise, with Islam, in the seventh century. During the eighth century, when the Zoroastrians fled Persia to escape conversion to Islam, Zoroastrianism also joined the colloidal dispersion of religions in India.

India has also given birth to its own religions: Hinduism from the Vedic times, Buddhism and Jainism from the third century BCE, and Sikhism during the sixteenth century.

After the terrorist attack on the Taj Mahal Hotel in Mumbai in 2008, the management of the hotel arranged a prayer meeting for those felled by the terrorists. The thirty-two deceased employees belonged to as many as six faiths and the sensitive, inclusive prayer meeting was conducted by priests from all the religions.

Social Grouping

For millennia, traders and invaders have come to the Indian subcontinent in search of knowledge and wealth. Often, they have made India their home. Various corners of India abound with fascinating stories of immigrant communities that have integrated seamlessly while preserving their unique identities. For instance, the Moplahs of north Kerala are thought to have descended from Arab traders of the Hadramauth even before Islam was established. The Siddis of Gujarat and Karnataka are known to have arrived in the twelfth century as East African slaves. They now speak Gujarati and Kannada, and although they look different and live their own distinct lives, they are very much a part of the society around them. Hussaini Brahmins are a Mohyal community from the Punjab area, who practice Hinduism but also observe Muharram.

Felicity with Language

In India, we speak more languages than any other country – 22 major languages are written in 13 different scripts and there exist over 720 dialects. Other communities and nations also view their society as complex and diverse. An incident at Kuala Lumpur in 1976 is illustrative. During a presentation on Malaysia attended by one of the authors by an advertising executive introduced Malaysia as a highly complex society because its people spoke three or four languages and practised three or four religions. This will not appear complex at all to an Indian. Many scholars believe that Tamil is the oldest language in the world, and it is still spoken all over Tamil Nadu and across many parts of India. Although many Indian languages derive from Sanskrit, most of these are distinct in grammar, phonetics and modern evolution, and are yet influenced by the others. Foreign languages like Turkish, Arabic and Persian have been assimilated into Indian languages just as Indian languages have influenced foreign ones, including the English language which has adopted innumerable Indian words.

A majority of educated Indians typically speak more than one language – their own mother tongue, the official language Hindi, English or another Indian language. The linguistic part of the Indian brain is 'plastic', so when they go to other lands, they learn fast. K.V. Rao, now a Singapore national, recalls that he learnt French and English in Pondicherry where he was born. He spoke Telugu at home, but also had to learn Tamil, the language of the state surrounding Pondicherry.

S.N. Venkat, adjunct faculty at the Singapore Management University, marvels at how language can make an Indian feel like a foreigner within the country. When, for example, a Tamilian crosses the Tamil Nadu border into Karnataka, the signs are all in Kannada, none of which he can normally read, making the atmosphere initially quite foreign. This becomes even more acute if he travels to north India. This is true for someone from Karnataka or north India when they travel to other parts of India.

Superstitious and Intuitive Beliefs

In the West, public or institutional superstition was banished with the Enlightenment in the seventeenth century. However, many of the most important decisions in Western management are taken intuitively, despite all the appurtenances of rationality. For example, which candidate to appoint as a senior leader, which manager is showing potential, which target acquisition to focus on over others, and so the list goes on. In India, intuition and superstition co-exist with modern rationality. Indians rely a great deal on intuition or superstition in their business dealings, and they do not hesitate to admit it.

In India, institutional superstition, or sentiment, as we prefer to term it, is very important. For example, when J.R.D. Tata called Ratan Tata to inform him that he would succeed J.R.D., Ratan Tata was requested to keep the matter quiet. J.R.D., it turned out, wished to consult Ajit Kerkar, the chairman of Indian Hotels, about an auspicious date for the news to put in the public domain. Similarly, when Rallis India inaugurated its first captive solar plant to run its crop protection factory, auspicious dates were first ascertained by a priest. Such incidents abound in the Indian corporate world but would appear strange among corporates anywhere else.

The Sociology of India

The organization of societies in the past and the development of human relationships has influenced how people organized themselves to survive and progress at various points of time. The precise connection may still be unclear, but the possible connection cannot be dismissed. Without delving deep into the merits or demerits of social practices, philosophical thought leadership, the evolution of the caste system, the political relationship between the king and his people, and the osmotic influences of spirituality, music and dance, we can see that they all influence how society organizes itself.

In the Western way of thinking, the king of an empire owned all the land and, along with the pope, was the representative of God on earth. That was never the case in the Indian way of thinking. In the latter, the king was merely a *bhaagidaar*, a shareholder of one-sixth of the produce. With the collection of this share, the king was required to deliver civic amenities and common facilities for the citizens. The local panchayats were the keepers of religious and social decorum and the arbiters of justice. Panchayats were decentralized and operated in a community or village as a whole.

Historians state that through the thirty centuries of recorded history of the Indian subcontinent, there has remained a sense of having a common tradition – gods, rituals, social practices – established through sharing of pilgrimages, religions and festivals. India, it can be said, was designed to be decentralized. This may be why the scholar-statesman C. Rajagopalachari referred to India as the world's 'only governmentless civilization.'

Trading Practices

In the pre-modern era of the world trading order, India had a primary place in international trade. Much has been written about the Angus Maddison analysis of India's pre-eminent share of the world GDP between 1 CE and 1000 CE. Less known and analysed are the strong trading traditions and systems of trading practised by Indians while establishing their global business networks. For example, the money exchange systems followed the Multani traders into Central Asia, the credit evaluation methods of the Kutchi Bhatias that travelled to the Middle East and Africa, and the training methods of the Chettiars that made their way to South East Asia. A number of fascinating accounts by business historian Professor Dwijendra Tripathi, who has written and taught extensively on the subject, and the The Story of Indian Business series mentioned earlier expose the reader to a breathtaking array of facts in this regard.

■

Since this is not a book on sociology, the facts briefly touched upon above might be enough to emphasize the point that in India – more than anywhere in the world – multiple religions, language groups and communities coexist while maintaining their own identity. It is not easy to accomplish this colloidal feat and in most countries there has been fierce homogenization either through religious conversion (like the Spanish Inquisition) or a common language (like the adoption of English in America) or ethnic congruence (like the Han Chinese).

Although India is a market of 1.3 billion people, a more accurate way of viewing the country is to see it as being comprised of 4,000 social groups of 300,000 individuals each on an average. Marketers understand this very well and use this knowledge while strategizing for their products. For instance, washing dishes with a liquid soap in a basin was, for a long time, unacceptable because of the prevalence of the concept of *jhootha* – though things might have changed in recent years. Branded tea sold in India has a different formulation in different parts of the country, based on the preferred local taste, which has been mapped by tea companies. The cooking oil used in the east of the country is mustard, whereas in the south it is coconut or sesame oil. Frozen foods have still not taken off in India despite many multinationals and Indian companies attempting to develop the market for the primary reason that a distribution deep freezer will not be permitted to store fish or meat along with frozen vegetables.

Since Indians are intuitively colloidal in their social relationships, they adapt very well wherever they go. Colloids in chemistry require a very high degree of particulate differences concurrently with mutual compatibility. In addition, colloids work on nature's principle of soft equilibrium – networking, diversity, redundancy, collaboration and adaptation.

Since chemistry teaches us that colloids have their own methods of stability, it leads us to wonder whether the colloidal nature of Indian society (and made-in-India managers) imparts a singular quality to their approach to problem-solving. What is indeed distinctive is the competitive intensity that the Indian student has to encounter while pursuing academics while growing up in India and that is what we will address in the next chapter.

4 AN ATMOSPHERE OF INTENSE COMPETITION

'I have been up against tough competition all my life. I wouldn't know how to get along without it.'

– Walt Disney

AS AUTHORS, WE ARE BOTH UNIQUELY QUALIFIED TO WRITE about the made-in-India global manager because we are the products of some of India's best engineering and management institutes with many years of corporate leadership and teaching experience to draw on. Many of the people that we have studied and worked with are already made-in-India global managers, and our own experiences and interactions with them underlie much of our conviction in our hypothesis.

Additionally, and perhaps more importantly, as professionals who are closely associated with educating and mentoring future Indian managers, we understand the pressures, trials and tribulations that these individuals face and what their strengths are. India is one of the most populous countries in the world, and as per World Bank statistics (2017) the population density in India is 150 times that of Australia and more than three times that of the US. This implies that the competition for resources and opportunities is intense. From getting admission into a coveted engineering or medical college to getting a clerical job in a government bank, Indian students learn early on that they have to be at their very best to access opportunity and, consequently, financial security. People talk about warriors being battle-hardened; having faced many intense battles just to get the opportunity to occupy a managerial position, the made-in India manager is prepared and shaped in many ways for success at the highest levels.

Competitive Intensity and Its Manifestation

The premier institutes the authors are associated with, including IIM Calcutta and SPJIMR, regularly host exchange students from equivalent business schools in Europe. Recently, SPJIMR conducted an informal focus group with ten such students to understand their perceptions of management education in India. Through the interviews, one of the consistent themes that emerged was the perception the foreign students have of Indian students being industrious and diligent. 'They are much more focused,' they said. 'It is very important to Indian students that they do well. We have become more hard-working by being around them. They are very competitive.'

This is an interesting insight because these students had themselves been selected to top business schools, and qualified for a sought-after exchange programme on the basis of their performance in class. Person for person, they felt that the Indian students were more determined, more focused and very hard working. Statistics bear this out. The State Bank of India, India's premier public-sector bank, recently advertised for entry-level probationary officers. It received, on an average 550 applications for every position available (*Times of India*, May 2018). This demonstrates that intense competition is not only for elite academic institutions but cuts across economic and social strata.

Currently, 1.2 million students take the entrance examination to the IITs, which have fostered a number of luminaries. As per a newspaper report in the *Hindustan Times* in 2017, Only 11,000 students were admitted to the IITs in 2017, an admit ratio of less than 1 in 100. India's foremost business school, IIM Ahmedabad, admits one student for every 400 applications. This makes it significantly more difficult to gain admission into than the business schools at Stanford (6 per cent acceptance rate) and Harvard (11 per cent acceptance rate), as per data sourced from the schools at www.poetsandquants.com.

What impact does a high degree of competition for opportunities across the board have on the preparation and mindset of the made-in-India manager?

Our Choices Shape Us in Many Ways

In the 1970s and 1980s, the career choices available to a promising student were limited and typically defined at an early stage in their lives. A student who was proficient in science and mathematics aspired to become a doctor or an engineer, and a student who opted for the commerce stream aspired to become a chartered accountant. At the undergraduate level, this typically meant that you had to do well in competitive examinations, and your status (and your family's status) depended upon your ability to make it through competitive examinations like IIT-JEE or to have the high marks required for admission into premier medical colleges.

For a child growing up in this environment, a couple of things became apparent quickly. First, while competition and scarcity of opportunity were inevitable aspects of life, you had to couple intelligence with a very high level of diligence if you were to make it to the next level and earn the approval of both your family and society. Secondly, you had a very limited number of acceptable choices of career and subjects of study, and your interests were largely defined from within this limited portfolio of choices. In addition, if you grew up in a metropolitan city, your exposure to coaching classes, the right books for study preparation and a set of competitive peers implied you were more aware of what it took to succeed in competitive exams than your peers in smaller towns such as Nagpur or Pune or Chandigarh.

The late 1970s and early 1980s were also the period when television was beginning to make its presence felt. The choice of programmes was restricted to the state broadcaster. In terms of the economic environment, product choices were also still restricted and competition limited. Cars were only made by Hindustan Motors (the iconic Ambassador) and Fiat, and two-wheelers by Bajaj.

We did have access to foreign books (many of us drew our images of the West from the writings of Enid Blyton, Franklin W. Dixon, Agatha Christie, P.G. Wodehouse and the like) and the West seemed removed from the restricted world that we were growing up in. These impressions were heightened by the foreign films we watched. The cars and the scenery they portrayed pointed to a life that was apparently so much better than the restricted and dreary world we were growing up in. When family members travelled abroad on work, each trip meant that children would aspire to possess international clothing and confectionery brands, a novelty in India at the time.

How did this affect the made-in-India manager? It led to a longing for, and an attraction to, all things Western, which in most cases, meant all things American. In many ways, it was at the heart of our American dream, and drew many of us to foreign shores. In *The Other One Percent: Indians in America*, the authors Sanjoy Chakravorty, Nirvikar Singh and Devesh Kapur, point out that Indian immigrants (who constitute one per cent of the US population) are the wealthiest and most successful immigrant group in the US. They write that the trend of the exceptional success of Indian immigrants began in 1965, when US immigration policy started placing an emphasis on technical skills and academic achievement, as well as family connections within the US, as criteria by which people could immigrate.

The success of Indian immigrants abroad is often attributed to the intensity involved in being a successful product of hyper-competitive stress. Competition for opportunity requires intensive focus on the ends and the means required to achieve them under stress, and this, in itself, builds a certain ability to focus.

Beginning with the End in Mind

Daniel Goleman is a bestselling author, thinker and researcher, perhaps known most for his work on emotional intelligence. In 2013, Goleman wrote *Focus* to highlight a relatively unexplored dimension of success: attention. Goleman explains that attention is controlled by the neo-cortex, a 'top down' brain function that helps us screen out distractions and focus our energies on a single task or thought. The essential component of the theory of focus is that the ability to develop selective attention in the midst of distraction builds 'a special wiring in the neo-cortex', an ability to inhibit emotion. Thus, people who focus best are 'able to stay on an even keel despite life's emotional waves.' It is in this context that we must re-examine our Indian upbringing.

Many Indians are brought up as a part of a salaried middle class, and the one thing that stands out through our lives is the importance that is attached to education – parental pride is linked to our academic performance. Scarcity and competition are facts of life, and even without being explicitly told every Indian child knows that we have to do really well academically if we are to make it to the best colleges. A lot of things are inculcated in the process – the importance of challenging work; practice as a tool of consistent success; understanding the pattern of an examination; and evolving an exam-oriented pattern of study.

It is still common for Indian students to prepare for competitive examinations by solving question papers from past examinations. In doing so, students learn early that the approach to success lies in evolving a clear understanding of what is being measured (and how) and tailoring their effort to the systems of measurement. Implicit in this practice is the reliable notion that there are a limited number of ways in which students can be questioned on a topic, and with the right preparation, the past could also predict the future. The idea of focused, goal-oriented practice has always been seen as a critical determinant of success, and been extensively tackled by a well-known self-help classic written by Steven Covey.

In 1988, Steven Covey wrote *The Seven Habits of Highly Effective People* in which he stated that the second of these seven habits is to 'begin with the end in mind'. This implies identifying a clear goal and making tangible progress towards the goal. Our best institutions (both leading institutions and reputed private coaching classes) have taken this thought to the level of a science. Focused preparation towards a structured goal, with dedicated, goal-oriented practice is second nature to an Indian student by the time they finish high school. The tangible skills of goal orientation, analysis and planning, tracking and continuous improvement through practice, are imbibed for life. It is no surprise to find that even an average product of this system often ends up being an exceptional academic performer in a foreign country.

Two Routes to Being a Global Manager

The made-in-India global manager has usually followed two routes to the US, where they have found their greatest success in that environment. In the first instance, these managers completed a foundational undergraduate or postgraduate degree in India, and then went to the US for higher studies. In the 1980s, nearly 50 per cent of the engineering students at institutes like the IITs or BITS Pilani opted to go abroad for a master's degree. This degree often led to employment at US companies such as Ford, General Motors, AT&T Bell Labs, and so on. Some Indians also followed up an undergraduate degree with a management degree from institutes like the IIMs, and then got a job with a multinational company in India. After working for the company for some time, the career path offered to promising young managers gave them international exposure, which they then leveraged to achieve global success.

As a variant of this path, some worked in India after graduation for a few years (often in an area related to an undergraduate specialization) and then went to the US to pursue management studies and a subsequent international career. In either of these cases, these were people who had, by the time they left Indian shores, overcome competitive odds of 1:50 or more on more than one occasion. When confronted with the difficulties of rising to the top of a global corporate ladder, they were unlikely to get fazed – they would merely dig in their heels and try harder. They had beaten much tougher odds before. Many things have changed since then, but this one thing has not. The competition for admission to the best institutes in India is fierce, and only the very best make the cut.

The Evolution of Competitive Intensity

In the present, while some things have changed significantly, others have not. One trend that has significantly evolved is that the number of students coming to premier institutes from Tier 2 and Tier 3 cities has gone up significantly. This is largely because of access. Good-quality English schooling and coaching classes have expanded beyond the metropolitan cities. Further, a student from these cities has equal access to modern media and international programming.

Cable television is available in all these cities, and early access to the Internet implies that gaps in awareness have narrowed.

These differences are still visible in students. While students from the metropolitan cities and traditional, elite schools have the advantage of wider exposure, and often speak a better quality of English, students from other cities come from more humble backgrounds, and have a fierce desire to do well and upgrade themselves. For them education is not merely a path to success, but a means to lift their families to a higher standard of living.

The number of high-quality education options available to the Indian student within the country has also increased significantly. Today, world-class institutions in the fields of law, design, architecture and fashion have been established across the country. Private universities like Ashoka University offer liberal arts courses with a wide variety of course options. However, the rise of these options has also been accompanied by an increase in population in particular cities and, with the expansion of awareness to centres outside the big cities the competition for admission to top institutions in India continues to be intense.

In recent years, the Indian government has attempted to expand the number of quality institutions in sought-after areas like engineering and management. In 2009, there were only seven IIMs, but as many as thirteen new IIMs have been established in the last seven years, many of them in smaller towns like Ranchi, Udaipur, Sambalpur, Kashipur, Bodh Gaya and Rohtak. While they will take time to build a strong faculty and stabilize, the access to quality education has broadened, and awareness and aspiration has spread to new catchments. Somewhere down the line, the number of high-quality would-be managers from India will increase. It is also interesting to note that the top institutes have maintained their standing, and despite an increase in the number of seats, it is more difficult to gain admission to IIM Ahmedabad or IIT Mumbai than it was ten years ago in terms of pure selectivity.

There are also other positive directions in which the student pool is moving. In 1989, when one of the authors (Ranjan) graduated from IIM Calcutta, the proportion of girls in the batch was lower than 10 per cent. In 2017, this figure is up to 31 per cent for IIM Calcutta (*Times of India*, June 2017). In a premier institute like SPJIMR in Mumbai, in 2017, 100 girls were admitted out of a total intake of 240 students. A more diverse student pool (both in terms of geography and gender) and a greater awareness due to early Internet exposure suggest that the made-in-India manager of tomorrow will be better prepared for a global environment.

However, there is some cause for caution. Today the desire to 'keep up with the Joneses' and constant comparison implies that, in many respects, students seem to be more insecure than they were in the past. Social media, with its stress on being liked, and public sharing of achievements, intensifies day-to-day comparison and thus amplifies competition. When students come to a premier institution, some of them quickly realize that they will no longer find it easy to stay at the top of the heap and they have difficulty accepting this reality. Additionally, millennials entering the workplace today have been brought up in post-liberalization India and, hence, have always seen an India where choice is ubiquitous and opportunities are abundant. This is perhaps one of the causes of a sense of entitlement within them, greater than was seen in previous generations.

However, this has a positive flip side. The Indian student today has grown up in an India that is perceived as a potential superpower. In sports like badminton, hockey, cricket, chess and billiards, and now also in boxing, wrestling and track-and-field Indians have demonstrated that they compete with the best. Indian managers have visibly risen to the top of global companies and several well-documented success stories are clear symbols of the made-in-India manager's ability to compete on a world stage. The awareness of their abilities and skills is greater in today's managers, largely because of the generation of role models who have shown the way.

As seen in this chapter, prospective Indian managers are perceived by their counterparts as focused, competitive and hard-working. They have seen and overcome large odds throughout their lives, and have realized the value of hard work and focused practice. The manager of tomorrow is from a more diverse background, and has already been through multiple layers of selection before he or she enters a top corporation. The individual is also more aware, self-confident and prepared to compete with the best in the world.

While competitive intensity can be a driver of success, it must also translate into a deep desire to learn and grow and inculcate the hunger to build. But this desire is equally a consequence of the moulding of personality and values that occurs by demonstration. A lot of this happens inside the home and is due to the influence of the family. To understand Indian managers better, we must thus understand the formative role their families play in their lives.

5 THE INFLUENCE OF THE FAMILY

'A family is a place where minds meet one another.'

– Gautama Buddha

MANAGEMENT IS THE ART AND SCIENCE OF GETTING THINGS done by means of people and processes. It is a science because there is a role for measurement and the systematic use of analysis and data, and there are some overriding principles that can be applied across contexts. It is an art in that it involves dealing with people in individual and group settings. There is significant role for understanding emotions within a team as well as substantial scope for tailoring actions to the personality and style of the individual manager. If we talk of a left brain, which is analytical and deals with facts and logic, and a right brain, which is more visual, deals with emotion and is capable of a more fluid intelligence and of thinking beyond rigid structures, then today's manager (and the manager of tomorrow) needs to be whole-brained.

In the sense in which we have defined management, it should be clear that the practice of management is observed frequently in day-to-day life. It equally means that even before students are exposed to any formal education in management they have been a witness to and a participant in the practice of management. The need to get things done is a feature of everyday life – in our families, schools and colleges, communities and friends' circles, and religious and cultural groups.

A large proportion of the formative managerial exposure of made-in-India managers are shaped by experiences within the family. It is the first informal organization they are is exposed to, and it shapes their values and beliefs. Many of their habits are learned by observation and imitation and, often, competitive intensity and a nurturing family with high expectations combine to create a hunger to build – the desire to create a future that is dramatically different from the present and past, and to develop a capability that is significantly ahead of the competitive set. Since this hunger often has its roots in the family, it is useful to examine some experiences that illustrate the way family can shape our outlook as leaders and managers, and then extend the argument to examine the role played by families in shaping the managers of today and tomorrow.

Learning from Our Parents

A lot of what we learn from our parents is tacit. It is learnt through observation, demonstration and daily shared experiences. Some habits are learned without being aware of the learning. It may reflect in the way you tear a chapatti, the sequence in which you eat a meal, or the order of your routine immediately after you wake up in the morning. At a fundamental level, your values and attitudes are in many ways shaped by your parents.

Self-Belief and the Magic of Lofty Expectations

Self-confidence is built by achievement in the face of obstacles. Often, a building block is early and unconditional caring in the immediate environment. Achievements in the student phase build self-confidence in academic domains and a relative lack of self-awareness in others. The managerial workplace has a new set of rules – and early failures, coupled with a supportive culture, helps managers to understand themselves, understand failure and, through experience, realize that learning from yesterday's failure builds today's success. They then develop a deeper confidence. It is a quiet self-belief, a feeling that says, 'If I am interested in something and want to make a difference, and I am willing to give it all my effort, then there is very little that I cannot prima facie achieve.' It does not need to be stated – it is a quiet determination and the ability to stay steadfast when short-term outcomes do not align with expectations. It is not a common quality, and we do not think it is inborn. Our managers typically achieve this in a mid-career phase, and those who get there earlier are often early leaders.

How did we get this from our parents? We believe Indian parents have always had high expectations. Children are expected to do well, and they are placed in an environment of intellectual challenge, encouraged to ask questions and read. This is mirrored in a childhood experience of one of the authors, Ranjan. In his words, 'During my childhood, we had the entire *Encyclopaedia Britannica* at home at a time when we chose not to possess a television. We were expected to do extremely well in school, but the larger message was, "We believe in you and your abilities." In your formative phases, this belief can be critical.

'In some ways, my academic choices were born out of an experiment – my father was convinced that formal schooling began too early. Consequently, I never went to kindergarten and started straight in the first standard. From the stories that my mother shares, it is apparent that my appetite for learning was much higher before I started school. Many years later, when I was working, my father shared this perspective, and I, true to form, said, "But wasn't it a risk? Would this work for the average student?"

'His response was, "We always knew you were not average." It was strangely reaffirming, this statement. The cynic would say that there is no parent who believes their child is average. Parents, by implicit and explicit behaviour, signal to the child that they do or not have confidence in them. One of the paradoxes of life is that we need to build self-belief to the extent that no single opinion can hurt us or elevate us. But we need consistent affirmation to get to the point where this is largely true. This is the role that parents play. Having a stable, nurturing family with high expectations creates an enabling environment crucial to building self-belief.'

These subjective experiences are not isolated. They are reflected in the memories of globally renowned made-in-India managers. Many of our contemporaries head corporations in and outside the country. When asked how growing up in India helped them, they emphasize the formative role of family, and speak with affection about the unconditional love of a parent, the confidence boost provided by a family member during a difficult phase, and the enduring encouragement of learning and reading. Dining-table conversations, even if passively observed, leave a strong impact on an individual's values and beliefs.

Anand Mahindra, one of India's most respected leaders, talked about his father's influence in an interview to *Forbes* magazine in 2016. His father was a businessman who went on to enter politics. The principle quality he recalls of his father is that of being 'a people person'. He goes on to say that his father's outstanding characteristic was humility. In Mahindra's own words (cited from the same *Forbes* interview), 'If you aren't humble, whatever empathy you claim is false, and probably results from arrogance or the desire to control.' We have had the opportunity to watch Mahindra dealing with his team, and he exemplifies humility in his ability to ask questions, listen and include employees across levels in any conversation.

Both Indra Nooyi, former chairman and CEO of PepsiCo, and Satya Nadella, presently the CEO of Microsoft, talk about the strong influence that their mothers have had on their upbringing, aspirations and values. The Indian middle class student has typically grown up in an extremely stable family environment, which has in turn encouraged high aspirations and deep self-confidence. Satya Nadella says of his mother, 'My mother cared deeply about my being happy, confident and living in the moment without regret.' Indra Nooyi talks about the things her mother did to help her daughters believe that they could 'become whoever they wanted to be.'

In a specific instance, Indra Nooyi recounts how her mother would ask both her daughters to make a presentation at the dinner table on what they would do if they were a particular world leader. She would then declare a winner. This kind of role-playing left a lasting impression on Nooyi.

Family environments in India are often characterized by a significant pressure to perform academically. Where these pressures come to bear in an environment which encourages curiosity, demonstrates belief in the child with shared aspirations, it becomes a strongly positive and formative force, and can lead to the child developing self-belief. It must be stated in fairness, that there are many families in which performance pressure and the freedom to ask questions do not go together and, in those cases, the family influence may have an adverse impact on a child's self-esteem. India is still a largely patriarchal society, and while this is beginning to shift slowly, our formative family influences are greatly shaped by the selfless service, discipline and commitment of that strongest of all institutions – the Indian mother.

An Abundance of Presence

In our patriarchal society, it is often true that a mother's exclusive focus is on bringing up her children and constantly encouraging them to be their best. The presence of at least one parent in the house at all times is an extremely stabilizing factor for children, to the point of being something that could be taken for granted. This gives us an anchor in relationships. Knowing and experiencing people who are worthy of trust in our daily lives gives us the ability to trust others. High self-esteem, self-belief and an understanding and appreciation of the worth of close relationships acts as strong foundations for us to understand ourselves and build deep connections.

Inclusivity and the Role of the Extended Family

The idea of family in India is rarely restricted to the immediate family. Even as nuclear families become stronger and more prevalent, we have the tendency to have large family get-togethers, celebrate achievements for each member and come together when a member of the extended family needs help. This notion of the extended family is strongly built during childhood. One of the authors (Ranjan) shares this experience from his childhood.

'While growing up in Mumbai, this notion of a large family was easily extended to visiting relatives and friends from our home town in West Bengal. If guests came at short notice, or if there was a shortage of essentials, or when somebody fell ill, adjustments were made, and they were made quickly. As children, we knew that we had to give up our bedroom for guests and share a mattress on the floor with others. Since this sacrifice was often accompanied by a heightened sense of excitement and activity around the house, we grew to welcome it. We also learned that guests were to be quickly included within the larger circle of family, and guests reciprocated by helping around the house.'

This form of inclusiveness, the ability to make strangers feel at home in a short period of time, is a huge learning in the formative years and it breeds a very different capacity for connections. Flexibility, the ability to make do with what you had, and a significant sense of cooperation and family cohesion were inculcated deeply. This profound sense of inclusivity and treating a guest as a family member is identified today as a defining characteristic of Indian hospitality – *atithi devo bhava* – and its origins can be traced to the inclusivity and hospitality of the Indian family.

Respect and Deference to Age

At a family gathering in India, younger people will often greet elders by touching their feet. There is deference to age and experience, and while it is sometimes merely ceremonial, this respect for age is reflective of a collaborative family environment. Elders are looked after and, unlike in the West, it is still quite common to see parents living with their children and grandchildren, which results in a far greater connectedness between generations. It is also a valuable way for society to utilize the wisdom of elders. This respect for seniority and experience can, in the right circumstances, keep an individual humble, if adapted meaningfully to the modern world. A young management trainee coming into a large corporation often has to learn the ropes from a senior field supervisor, someone with twenty years of experience and seniority in both age and wisdom. The challenge is to learn from the senior, and then acquire acceptance as a leader of the same individual. This implies humility and respect at the individual level, which is irrespective of the individual position. It is then backed by the realization that the young manager may never become a better field supervisor than the senior, but can enable the supervisor to become a better version of himself.

Adaptation to the modern world requires the ability to blend this respect with an ability to question. A combination of personal respect and professional, issue-based dissent will ensure, to quote a phrase that was popularized by one of the authors (Gopal), that we are able to 'disagree without being disagreeable'.

The Role of Religion and Spirituality

Many of us have been brought up in environments where one or both parents were deeply religious. Prayer is often an important part of life in India, and as satirized in films like *3 Idiots* we often pray harder when we seek a specific outcome in a given situation. While religion, taken to the extreme, can have negative consequences, the concept of a higher being, implicit long-term rewards for doing the right thing and staying true to your principles are often linked to our exposure to religion. The formative stories from Indian mythology (often stories of gods and their incarnations) do a lot to build a sense of right and wrong. The concept of servant leadership, first articulated by Robert Greenleaf in 1970, talks about leaders serving those below them and, in a sense, achieving outcomes, by enabling others to achieve their goals. Vineet Nayyar, former chief executive of HCL Technologies, talked about putting employees first and customers second, and suggested that since frontline employees were the true point of customer contact, the organization should be viewed as 'an inverted pyramid', with each person serving the level below. With tangible examples, he demonstrated that using this approach was crucial to HCL's success story. This notion of a servant leader is echoed in the *Bhagavad Gita* and the *Arthashastra* – 'in the happiness of his subjects lies his happiness, in their welfare his welfare'.

These values are not only talked about, but they are also demonstrated. In class, when students are asked to state a couple of values which are dear to them, and how and when they acquired that value, it is often not easy for them to identify, but after introspection, what emerges is the personal story of a family member, an example of personal sacrifice or caring in difficult circumstances which set an enduring example. Allow us to share a story.

In 1989, when one of the authors (Ranjan) completed his MBA in 1989, a classmate employed with a prestigious foreign bank shared with him that his starting salary was higher than the salary his father had retired with. He did this not with boastful pride, but with heartfelt emotion and deep gratitude. He had seen the sacrifices his father had made to give him the opportunities he'd had, and an important part of his ambition was a desire to live up to his father's sacrifice and aspirations.

Thus, we can see that for today's manager, the sense of security and well-being, the deeper sense of duty and ethics, the ability to be inclusive and the hunger to succeed are all, to an extent, driven by the influence and sacrifice of the family. However, as time passes, parenting styles and the role of the extended family are changing rapidly, family influences differing in many ways for tomorrow's managers.

There are many things that endure, though. A well-knit family environment, a keen sense of right and wrong, the presence of formative and strong family influences and a hunger to upgrade themselves and their families are still visible. These factors are coupled with a greater and broader social awareness, a willingness to explore multiple passions and a rejection of hierarchy for its own sake. If backed with a positive attitude, this can be a heady combination. Managers will not always get the results they want. The ability to introspect, take feedback from others, and use each result to improve the process is at the heart of good attitude. In recent times, former captain of the Indian cricket team M.S. Dhoni is a great example – in defeat or success, his equanimity is similar, he never shirks personal responsibility, and his focus is always on 'ways to improve the process'. The right attitude is contingent on the manager's ability to understand herself or himself fully, because we cannot improve that which we cannot understand and accept.

6 THINKING IN ENGLISH, ACTING IN INDIAN

'Those who cannot express what they have learnt are like flowers without fragrance.'

– Thirukkural

THE CHALLENGE OF MANAGING LARGE ORGANIZATIONS SPREAD to the East effectively only after the Second World War. This brought in a cultural overlay in management thinking in the West. However, these learnings did not require any change in the behaviour of Western managers in their own social contexts.

So, while for the Western managers there is an Eastern cultural overlay on their management thinking, for Eastern managers there is a Western intellectual tradition as an overlay on the Eastern social context. This gives rise to attitudinal and behavioural patterns that are vastly different. For example, Anglo-Saxon cultures over the years tended to view a company as a system, whereas Eastern cultures tended to see them as a social group. It is little wonder that Anglo-Saxon thinking has strongly influenced advancements in productivity management through time and motion study, system dynamics, and so on. Eastern thinking, on the other hand, has strongly influenced advancements in human motivation management.

Indian managers, however, are different from their counterparts in other emerging countries. Most of them think, verbalize, articulate and gesticulate in English at an almost frenzied pace. In case the reader has any doubt about the veracity of this statement, a single evening spent watching an Indian English-language television channel will expose you to the inspired invectives of Indians who think in English. If you seek efficient expression in the English language, you will be disappointed; if, however, you seek effectiveness in the delivery of the message, it will be visible and palpable.

Efficiency versus Effectiveness

This chapter is predicated on a premise mentioned earlier in the book – that management results are derived from two vectors: the first is the thinking or intellectual vector, and the second is the action or transactional vector.

The thinking vector is influenced by the power of analysis, exposure to media and books, and the language of thinking. The transactional vector is influenced by culture, social mores and the arc of acceptable behaviour. These vectors in turn tie into the concepts of efficiency and effectiveness. Effectiveness and efficiency are not the same thing. A fly approaches a pot of honey in spiral circles. This is an effective method for the fly, given its anatomy, though flying in a straight line would have been more efficient. In the workplace, this distinction manifests itself in typical Indian ways.

In Western cultures, it is efficient to speak one after the other, just as it is to stand in a queue or not honk at the vehicles ahead of you. In India, effectiveness is seen to be achieved by getting noticed. There is thus a tendency to interrupt others while speaking, jump queues and honk relentlessly even when it is quite evident it will not help anyone move an inch further. From a Western viewpoint, this is sheer bad manners and indiscipline, but it is considered quite all right in the Indian way of thinking. The fact is that this is a cultural difference and not related to education or the economic status of the country because even the most educated Indians indulge in these behaviours. More remarkably, these behaviours manifest themselves most strongly within the country and Indians rarely indulge in them when travelling abroad!

English has been adopted as the national language or the dominant language of the administration and business not only in the UK, Australia–New Zealand (Australasia) and North America, but also in India. Soon, India will have more English speakers than in the UK, Australasia and Canada put together. As the second-largest English-speaking nation in the world, interesting and unintended consequences are emerging for India.

The Indian professional class is defined to include the government, civil and defence services, private-sector and public-sector business organizations, the IT sector, the banking and financial verticals, lawyers, accountants and doctors. At least half of these professionals have a high exposure to English through education, media, books and official practice. Over time, thanks to wider access to education, increased mobility, rapid urbanization and the perception that fluency in English advances careers, many professionals have acquired what we would term an exclusively 'English-language mindset'. That is, from merely speaking the language, they have begun to think in the language. While culture specialists may bemoan this development, in this chapter, we shall explore this reality and its consequences.

The World's Only Two-Vector Managers

We have travelled through many countries and observed that the managers in each country think in their mother-tongue and act in accordance with local cultural norms. English-speaking Japanese managers will converse quite slowly because when they receive an English message, they first translate it into Japanese, think through their response in Japanese, translate it back into English and finally voice their reply. Here, Japanese does not just refer to the language, but is rather reflective of the prevalent local societal and cultural norms and environment. This is true also of managers of other nationalities, such as Chinese, Indonesian and Arab.

On the other hand, most Indian business executives receive all of their business training in English, exclusively read English papers, watch English news channels, and quote the *Economist* and *Harvard Business Review*, Drucker and Adam Smith to express their point of view. This creates a class of professional managers who turn to English when they wish to articulate a complex thought – a phenomenon that is referred to throughout this chapter as 'thinking in English'. This is the intellectual vector of thinking.

Coming to the action or the transactional vector of management, when Indian executives operate in the Indian environment, the social dynamic and organizational politics are naturally rooted in Indian cultural norms. For example, Indian managers tend to think holistically rather than in parts, are deferential to their elders, do not voice dissent openly and give undue importance to seniority when all other things are equal. These are just some of the more noticeable behaviours among Indian professionals.

Thus, Indian managers are distinctive in that their business-thinking tradition is Anglo-American, but their action tradition is deeply rooted in Indian culture and values. This is unusual. Put simply, while Japanese (or Chinese or Arab) managers think and act in Japanese (or Chinese or Arabic), only Indian managers think in English and act in Indian!

The Implications for Work and Management

When the vectors of thought and action are aligned, you get the best possible combination of efficiency and effectiveness. The concept appears to be axiomatic, and three examples might help to illustrate the point.

First, if the mindset in an organization dictates that differences with senior colleagues must not be expressed openly, and that is aligned with the action vector, you can get an outcome that is effective and efficient within that context. Of course, that does not mean that the outcome is a good one. Take the case of Korean Air, which faced frequent air crashes between 1988 and 1998. When an enquiry was finally conducted it turned out that the chief pilot's social status was so high in Korean society that junior officers would usually be oblique in their communication with him, even in cases that required direct and urgent action. In many instances this led to dire consequences as co-pilots would simply allow the pilot to take major decisions even if they were questionable.

Second, under the leadership of Jack Welch, General Electric (GE) decided that a rigorous portfolio analysis with a transparent methodology was essential to enhance shareholder value. This mindset, combined with their capability for disciplined execution, delivered hugely positive outcomes which have been well documented.

Third, public-sector banks in India are known to have the persistent problem of non-performing assets (NPAs). Publicly available commentaries display a high level of skill in data-gathering, analysis and policy options, but the execution of those ideas gets bogged down in socio-cultural issues such as a politician–businessman nexus, deference to authority and an orientation towards relationships rather than discipline when it comes to making decisions.

What are the manifestations of a two-axis manager? How does it show up in business conduct? Here are some examples that illustrate the various ways in which Indian managers sometimes think in English but act in Indian.

For the first, we draw on one of the authors' (Gopal) personal experiences in corporate India.

'From my personal experience, I worked in Unilever for three decades and in Tata Sons for almost two. I survived and grew in both because I adapted to their unique cultures. My comments are not intended to suggest that one is superior to the other. The observations below are just what they are – they provide a contrast.

'Unilever is highly process-oriented and goal-driven in articulating ambitions and getting things done. It is very Anglo-American in its approach in that it tries to cut out unnecessary issues around a problem, focus on the essentials and address relevant issues efficiently. Unilever neither encouraged nor tolerated ambiguity; in fact, the organization did all it could to distance itself from ambiguity.

'In contrast, Tata Sons is very Indian and highly relationship-oriented. Goals are relatively fuzzy and the accountability of getting things done is not always clear. While an analytical approach is encouraged, it provides room for ambiguity and accepts the view that the problem need not be stripped to its bare bones. The space to take a more holistic view of the many related issues surrounding the task is always present.

'At Unilever and Tata Sons, I experienced two similar disciplinary cases with different outcomes. At Unilever, a long-serving field supervisor was proven to have fudged his expense statement for a small sum. He had travelled in a lower-class compartment in a train, but had claimed a higher-class fare. The investigation system worked with finesse, and after all the facts were gathered and the supervisor was given the opportunity to explain himself, he was fired. The thinking vector stated that dishonesty is what it is, regardless of how much money was involved. The action vector had to be consistent with this.

'At Tata Sons, an employee inflated a medical claim by adding a zero to the top left of the 100-rupee expense incurred, making it appear like 900 rupees were spent. The matter was detected, the employee was confronted and a confession obtained. The decision on the punishment, however, went through a complex process of referrals, consultations and discussions. Finally, from a compassionate perspective, the employee was given a warning, denied two increments but allowed to continue working for Tata Sons.

'To take another example, both companies have a retirement age for employees. In Unilever, there are virtually no cases of extension of employment or post-retirement advisory positions. The thinking vector of the organization dictates that since there is no uncertainty about retirement, the management had best plan succession well.

'In Tata companies, cases of retirements being deferred or advisory positions created to extend terms of employment are far more frequent. The thinking vector here states that the person possesses valuable expertise, which will not dissipate after retirement, and may work to the benefit of the competition, so why not retain such expertise for a few more years?

'Given the cultures of the individual organizations, former Unilever executives regard themselves (on a voluntary basis) as alumni and behave like the alumni of an educational institution. They carry fond memories of their days at Unilever, maintain a few work friendships, demonstrate a benign interest in current events at the organization, but cut themselves off from it, which, for the most part, is actively encouraged. It is less so at Tata Sons. Former employees speak of their association with a sticky warmth, recall their own contributions and experience with great emotion and actively seek to know what is going on in the group after their departure. The organization also values former relationships and does not disassociate itself from former employees, though it is not necessarily welcoming of too much interest either, which is as it should be.'

Now take the instance of Infosys. As a company, Infosys is very proud of its humble Indian roots, established as it was by a few cash-strapped professionals who got together in 1981 to create a world-class IT services company. For them, their workplace and their enterprise was their temple, the software business was their religion, and though they were pursuing wealth for all it was subordinate to their morals (dharma). The founders were proud to maintain values of austerity, humility, respect for money and a single-minded focus on customer service. However, in terms of organizational efficiency, they were smart enough to adopt international benchmarks in organizational design, human-resource practices and corporate governance. Although they had mainly foreign customers during their first 20 years, they continued to provide their services from India, with Indian talent. However, a few things changed for the company once it was listed in NASDAQ.

It began with the leaders thinking and talking about going global. The company was presented as having an international flavour and foreign nationals were recruited into its workforce. European, American and non-resident Indian nationals were invited to join the board. Retirement and board-renewal policies were adopted from international practices; governance practices were benchmarked with international corporations. The humble and austere founders were now capitalist owners of considerable financial assets. Infosys was talked about as a paragon of transparent virtue, comparable to the best international corporations. It just happened to be of Indian origin. After the founders had all taken a sequential strike from the CEO crease, the board looked outside, not just in India but globally, to find a CEO. They found Vishal Sikka, the archetype of a made-in-India global manager.

Against all of this thinking in English, however, transactional anomalies typical to India will soon emerge. When it had come to CEO succession, the group of founders had acted like a family business, taking over sequentially from each other until they could not do so any more without seriously damaging the fibre and future of the company. For a couple of years, the patriarch of the company N.R. Narayana Murthy even inducted his son as his personal assistant – an anathema in a global corporation. On the other hand, Sikka, a professional manager, was hired at a much higher salary because he was Indian-American. When Sikka was introduced to the shareholders under the watchful eye of eager television crews, he did a very Indian thing: he advanced towards Murthy and bent to touch his feet! In a Western-oriented corporate environment, it was an amazing act of thinking in English and acting in Indian.

Murthy welcomed Vishal Sikka with the warmth that patriarchs are expected to display. With wide-eyed humour, he said, 'I understand Vishal means big, and Sikka means money. So now Infosys shareholders can expect big money through Vishal Sikka.' This was an expression of a very typical Indian sentiment, repeated when sons and grandsons seek the blessings of the elders before embarking on a career or business venture.

Encouraged by the English-thinking sentiments, the English-minded Sikka did English-minded things that any global CEO would do. But soon he found his feet caught up in the quagmire of the Indian action soil. Whispers, whistles, rumours, intrigue and exposure through the media started distracting the board and the management. Eventually, matters took a grave turn, resulting in Sikka quitting his post within three years of being at the helm.

We have so far seen the rich historical, cultural and individual influences that have shaped the Indian manager of today. To take our argument further and assess our claim that a series of factors come together in a constantly evolving way to make the made-in-India manager and thinker a force to reckon with in the future, we must first understand the forces that will shape the world of tomorrow and then situate a future made-in-India manager in this context.

7 THE MANAGER OF TOMORROW

'Leadership and learning are indispensable to each other.'

– John F. Kennedy

THE WAY WE MANAGE IS A FUNCTION OF OUR UPBRINGING, choices, exposure and the contexts in which we are required to function. There are changes in contexts across generations, and these impact both the family and the workplace. Here, we explore some of these changes and the ways in which they could shape managers of today and tomorrow.

The Made-in-India Manager of the Future is Different

Both the authors belong to a generation in which respect and authority of parental figures was unchallenged and dissent was rare. The current generation of parents has shifted to a less hierarchical style of parenting. This shift is a function of the influence of Western lifestyles and values along with, possibly, a desire for their children to grow up in a less exacting environment.

Western lifestyles are reflected in our enhanced awareness of Western entertainment, experience of foreign travel, a far greater emphasis on individual freedom and self-expression and the increased availability of global brands in our day-to-day lives. At a parental level, it often implies that the affluent Indian wishes to educate his child in an environment which is more open to questioning and exploration. The mushrooming of international schooling institutions across our cities is a testament to this shift. Thus, the generation of today has been brought up in a far more democratic way than those that have gone earlier, with a greater exposure to Western values that stress upon the importance of personal freedom and individualism. This implies a different balance between individualism and collectivism, and the willingness to question hierarchy and authority.

These differences are often amplified by the fact that today's manager is a 'digital native' – somebody who has grown up with technology deeply embedded in their upbringing. Information is easily available electronically and a lot of relationships are managed electronically. Often, this manager has to report to a digital migrant – somebody who did not grow up with technology, but has seen rapid differences in technology emerge after she or he entered the formal workplace.

Coupled with a wider set of available career and educational options, this is a generation which expects to be taught and led in a different way. While organizations will adapt to these changing expectations over time, an implication of this change in values is that these made-in-India managers are far less likely to be tolerant of hierarchical ways of functioning than their predecessors. This can cut both ways. On the one hand, it implies that this is a generation more attuned to dissent and possesses a natural bias for collaborative working, which should positively impact managerial styles in the workplace. On the other hand, it may lead to a lesser willingness to adapt to alternative styles, and this, coupled with impatience, could lead to higher attrition and consequently lower learning in each role. Expectations in the work environment are also impacted by the way employees choose to interact.

The ways in which we communicate and relate to one another are also changing. It is not uncommon to find people who live five minutes away from each other or even those who live together communicating through mediums like WhatsApp. Likes on Facebook and Instagram are the new ways in which people make connections and attention spans are significantly lower. So, how do the traditional Indian strengths of connecting and building relationships operate in the Facebook generation?

How Indianness has Evolved

As the generation that was directly or indirectly exposed to the Indian Freedom Movement, the parents of most managers of today have a sense of idealism and hope related to India and its future that their have children imbibed from them. While earlier generations were exposed (through books, comics like *Amar Chitra Katha* and popular television) to Indian mythology and were aware of stories from the Ramayana and the Mahabharata, it is our belief that the current generation is less connected with both Indian history as well as with the scriptures. Many have travelled abroad, and have a proper understanding of Western lifestyles and possibilities, but they do not really understand the heritage they come from.

On the positive side, this generation has grown up with an Indian cricket team that regularly wins games both within and outside India, sportspeople who compete globally and win, and Indian multinationals which are now global brands. They thus possess a greater confidence that India can take on the world and win. This affects their aspirations and self-belief positively, and mentally prepares them to compete with the best in the world. They are also willing to explore multiple interests and take risks. On the negative side, they may tend to be impatient with the weaknesses of an India that is still characterized by shaky infrastructure, corruption, strict hierarchies and bureaucracy.

To understand fully the manager of the future, we need to explore how workplaces have evolved and will continue to evolve. We live in an increasingly interconnected world, with access to information at our fingertips, an aware and demanding consumer market, and business models that are being redefined as we speak.

The Workplace of the Future

At the end of the Cold War, the U.S. Army War College coined the term VUCA (Volatility, Uncertainty, Complexity and Ambiguity) to describe the world at that point, and it has since taken root in the field of strategic leadership. VUCA, which is becoming a common management term today, is used to characterize the nature of the environment that managers operate in. Organizations themselves are evolving, and the workplace of the future must also evolve to thrive and prosper in a VUCA world.

Note that VUCA refers to the nature of the business environment – the context in which organizations operate. However, organizations themselves have been in flux. There has been a parallel shift in the nature of organizations that has helped them to adapt to a VUCA world.

In 2016, the Conference Board's Global Executive Coaching Survey conducted for that year coined the term BOCA (Blurred boundaries, work Overload, increased Complexity and Addiction to technology) to describe the workplace of the future – a workplace that is a response to a VUCA world. It is in this environment that the manager of tomorrow needs to thrive. Keeping this in mind, we must examine the BOCA model in greater detail.

Blurred Boundaries

Work is now increasingly performed across geographies and time zones. Within an organization, it is no longer necessary (or desirable) that an employee have a single line of reporting. A typical mid-level employee in a multinational corporation may have a functional boss for his core job, but will often also be working simultaneously as part of a regional or global team. Often, the individual is likely to be a part of a cross-functional team working across countries and time zones.

The definition of a workforce and the workplace are also blurring. The actual work that is done on a project may involve teams of full-time, contract and outsourced workers, and many of them may only communicate electronically. With members of a project team being situated across the globe, it is possible to have a team that responds to a project 24×7.

Technology, often seen as a support function within an organization, is now embedded in every business function. Implicitly, the industrial organization is transitioning to the digital organization and managers across levels and functions are required to have a less compartmentalized view of work. The realities of centralized storage and decentralized access to information tell us that it is now both possible and desirable for front-line employees to have far greater authority and visibility in an organization, especially when it comes to decision-making.

Communication boundaries are also getting increasingly blurred. A significant amount of information that concerns day-to-day organizational issues is shared through WhatsApp groups. The membership of these groups is task-dependent and can, hence, override conventional organizational boundaries. The fallout, of course, is that it is increasingly difficult to control information flow within and outside the organization, and the notion of information being restricted to certain layers of the hierarchy is equally hard to implement.

From all indications, eventually, the boundaries between 'human work' and 'machine work' will blur. With rapid evolution taking place in the fields of artificial intelligence, big data, robotics and cloud-based storage and processing, a number of jobs that have been seen as specialized human jobs may, in the future, be done by machines. Not only will there be a blurring of the human–machine possibility frontier, but this will also force managers towards a deeper reflection regarding the role and purpose of the modern organization and the role of technology within it.

The Limits of Human Attention

In 1972, the Club of Rome began a pioneering study on learning and its boundaries. Published in 1979 and titled *No Limits to Learning: Bridging the Human Gap*, the report spoke of the human gap as the 'gap between growing complexity and our ability to cope with it'. Universally, it seems that the amount of time spent reacting to short-term crises has gone up, as has workplace stress and the demand on personal time.

The variety of situations one confronts at work also seems to have increased. We have moved from unity of command (a single boss) to matrix organizations; from regular work hours to working across time zones; from one-to-one interaction to a multiplicity of communication modes across digital and offline media; and increasing demands to work across traditional functions and boundaries. As consumer demands become more complex and the intensity of competition grows, the demands on human beings to adapt and grow continuously is much greater. This, coupled with the evolution of technology and the need to adapt to newer ways of working, implies that sometimes experienced managers face greater challenges because they have to both unlearn and learn different ways of working. A range of organizations – from Infosys to McKinsey to Unilever – stress the importance of learnability in recruiting prospective managers. The manager of tomorrow must have the ability to continuously unlearn and learn.

Complexity (A World Out of Balance)

An increasingly materialistic world with strong competitive pressures, deepening complexity and time pressure, a constantly plugged in digital environment and the experience of rapid and unpredictable change often creates the perception of a life out of balance.

Noted management expert Henry Mintzberg has, in his latest book, provocatively titled *Rebalancing Society: Radical Renewal beyond Left, Right and Center*, argued that a democratic society should balance 'individual, collective and community needs, attending to each adequately but none excessively'. His central idea is that there are three arms of society – the private, the public, and the plural or social sector. He argues that a healthy democracy requires balance among these three arms and an over-dependence on any one arm creates an unstable society. He suggests that today too much power resides with large private organizations, and society cannot be sustainable or healthy if large private organizations engage in 'the unbridled pursuit of profit'.

This has implications for the modern organization. Managers of tomorrow must find a way to balance the needs of multiple stakeholders. The ability to cater to multiple stakeholders and see the world though multiple lenses implies the need for a far more flexible and self-aware manager. In this quest, technology can be both a boon and a hindrance.

Addiction to Technology

Ask a group of senior executives in a leadership retreat to stay away from their phones for half a day and you will be met with expressions of extreme discomfort. Some will even walk up to you privately and tell you about that urgent call that they just 'have to take'. However, when you confront them in a non-threatening moment and ask them what would happen if they were to actually be unavailable for a week, they confess that life in their organizations would go on rather well without them. An hour without a mobile phone eventually turns out to be relaxing, and some managers resolve to ditch their phones more often. It is clear that we have developed an exaggerated sense of our own importance and moved from being enabled by technology to being enslaved by it.

A large variety of digital communication media technologies means that there is a barrage of communication from multiple sources across multiple media. From the number of messages in our email inboxes to the many active chat groups on our smartphones, the urge to attend to a large volume of ongoing chatter, much of which is in the urgent but not important category, is almost overwhelming. We have less time for meaningful work and interaction and, as a result, we often feel stressed and overloaded. Coupled with workplaces that are less linear, and a new generation of millennial employees who expect more independence and greater agility, we feel a sense of change fatigue – that too much is changing too quickly and that many of one's capabilities may soon become unwanted or irrelevant.

The Way Forward

What, then, does tomorrow's manager need to do differently to prepare for the workplace of the future?

Unilever and Asian Paints are among a few companies that have spawned many successful corporate CEOs. Anand

Kripalu at Diageo, D. Shivakumar at the Aditya Birla Group and formerly at PepsiCo, Bharat Puri and Chandramouli Venkatesan at Pidilite Industries and Suresh Narayanan at Nestlé are all examples of successful chief executives who started their careers at one of these two wonderful companies. In a recent conversation, Bharat Puri offered an interesting insight into what set these managers apart. Essentially, companies like Unilever and Asian Paints have high recruiting standards, identify talented executives with strong values, and expose them to a variety of situations in which they get early responsibility and have the ability to perform. In doing so, they are supported by a company with strong systems and processes.

The critical thing that sets the best apart is that they are able to extend this understanding to situations where systems and processes are not in place. This implies an ability to understand contexts, assess the manager's current capabilities with regard to a new environment and identify areas of focus. As an example, if you are used to analysing information and taking successful data-driven decisions, and you move to an environment where the right data is not easily available, realizing this early will be both difficult and critical.

The ability to assess an environment and differentiate between those things which must be mastered and those which must be understood to an acceptable level is also important. Learning is not enough; knowledge must be used to change behaviours and ways of working for the better. Implicit in these tenets is the notion that we must begin to change the things that made us successful before they make us fail in the future. A manager must have the ability to assess, learn and assimilate, and to gauge a situation and adapt to it. Thus, learnability and adaptability are at the heart of success for managers in the future.

Learnability

The term 'lifelong learning' was introduced by Leslie Watkins in Denmark in 1971 in the context of learning inside and outside the classroom in formal education, but it is used far more frequently today. Learnability is at the root of lifelong learning and it can simply be defined as 'the ability to learn'. The *Oxford English Dictionary* defines the verb 'learn' as 'gain or acquire knowledge or skill in (something) by study, experience or being taught'. Learnability, however, goes beyond this definition – being able to learn requires a conscious attitude of awareness, reflection, humility and the ability to experiment.

The late Warren Bennis, founding chairman of the Leadership Institute at the University of Southern California, is widely regarded as one of the world's foremost thinkers on leadership and an early advocate for a more participative, collaborative and humble view of leadership. In Bennis's view, self-knowledge is at the heart of the effective leader and implies that you can separate 'who you are and who you want to be from what the world thinks you are and wants you to be.'

According to Bennis, the four tenets of self-knowledge are:

Be your own best teacher: One of the authors, (Ranjan) cites an example of a student who came to him after a class, saying that he wanted to pursue a career in marketing, but 'was not good at speaking in front of groups'. He was taken aback when he was asked, 'Is this [the inability to speak in front of groups] something you were born with?' The student was then told that public speaking was a learned skill. The idea was not to see it as a fait accompli, but a skill that could be learned through practice. The student in question went on to take this advice to heart, practised regularly (encountering with many failures along the way) and converted this apparent weakness into a strength.

For both students and managers, this implies shifting the focus to areas of personal action and not seeing abilities as 'cast in stone'. By taking decisive action, you can alter the gap between what you can do and what you aspire to do. This implies taking personal responsibility for both your education and day-to-day actions, and growing beyond blame ('other people are the problem') and denial ('I don't have a problem').

Accept responsibility; blame no one: A few years ago, one of the authors (Ranjan) was consulting with a company where the CEO complained of employees passing the buck, and continually and needlessly copying higher-level managers on emails. The CEO in question was indignant when told 'you are probably a part of the problem'. He was then asked whether he had actively and expressly discouraged his team members from needlessly copying him. This turned out to be a significant realization for the CEO and created a chain of demonstration down the line. The willingness to acknowledge that you may have had a role to play in problems that confront you, and beginning with self-analysis, is a rare quality and can be valuable in leading change.

You can learn anything you want to learn: This implies that if you aspire to greater things, you will have a willingness to take on new challenges. Strongly linked to innovator David Kelley's notion of 'creative confidence', this is a belief that the human mind can, through systematic unlearning and learning, build new skills and habits in areas of its interest. At a recent convocation ceremony at SPJIMR, one of us (Ranjan) asked a highly successful graduating student what difference the MBA course had made to him. In essence, the student's response was that he had realized that: a) he now had a fair exposure and understanding of multiple business domains and functions; b) going into the workplace, there was a lot he would not know; and, c) with the right attitude and openness, he was confident that he would be able to figure out the things he did not know.

Reflecting on your experiences: One of the authors (Ranjan) cites this example. 'One of the things I learned from my children was the habit of consciously saying thank you to the lift operator at our residence after every ride. One day, he started talking to me about his aspirations. I learned that he loved music, and after his shift, he played in a band. I realized that we often tend to take many people for granted and underestimate the truth that every human being likes to be acknowledged and has personal talents and aspirations.'

While the anecdote is compelling, the larger point is the need to learn from this specific experience and extend it to other relationships. This is where reflection comes in. Failure and success are inevitable, but the ability to separate outcomes from a realistic assessment of your role in creating that outcome requires the ability to fundamentally question yourself. This is a necessary condition for self-awareness and is essential for purposive action and personal growth.

Inculcating Learnability

What, then, are the right environmental conditions to foster learnability?

Aspiration and stretch: Being taught to question the status quo coupled with an upbringing which encourages children to aim high and work hard towards their goals enables young people to have aspiration and a strong work ethic. Often, education is seen as a passport to aspiration and this lays emphasis on formal learning. In India, aspiration and stretch are often seen as the desire to better one's material condition through education. Rajdeep Sardesai, the celebrated journalist and occasional quizmaster, once commented in a personal conversation that his experience in national-level quiz competitions suggested that children from Tier 2 and Tier 3 cities were aware, hungry and far more motivated than their counterparts from wealthy, big-city schools.

Competitive intensity: If aspiration is accompanied by an acceptance of competition as a fact of life, it leads to a willingness to measure oneself against external standards and work on bridging gaps. Competitive intensity also ensures that children experience failure and disappointment early on. Overcoming failure and disappointment to create further success breeds a more grounded and confident individual with a greater sense of self-worth. At a recent get-together of a premier engineering institute, an alumnus and successful venture capitalist shared that one of the things that had impacted him deeply was his entry into a premier educational institute. He quickly realized that there were others who were better than him in multiple dimensions, and the ability to accept this realization and yet build confidently on one's strengths reflected an important transition.

Peers, mentors and role models: A strong and stable family environment provides people with anchors around which they can build themselves. Values and character are better learned through observation and demonstration. A family environment that fosters discipline, integrity and the sense of living for each other builds emotional stability. Peers play an important role as well – they not only make one aware of one's strengths and shortcomings, but also provide a supportive community for individuals to learn and grow. Anil Sachdev, founder of Grow Talent and of the School for Inspired Leadership (SIOL), shared in a private conversation that when he asks leaders in Western countries to share who the influential role models in their lives are, it is very rare for them to name a parent or a family member. Conversely in India, almost all managers will cite the formative role played by a parent or family member in their lives – a lot of the value core of the Indian manager is derived from these role models.

Ambiguity: While one needs some anchors to be secure, experiencing unpredictability and surprise makes individuals less likely to take their environment for granted. Growing up in India, it is not uncommon to experience situations in which systems do not work. This could include situations where there is a power outage, a disruption in plans due to weather conditions, extremely large crowds getting to work, and more. Implicitly, we also learn that these situations can be handled and the way forward is to reassess and build a modified course of action. This, in itself, is a valuable preparation for a more ambiguous management context.

Attitude to failure: A society that encourages risk taking and experimentation does not attach stigma to failure. This gives young people the courage to try new things, and be personally and socially honest about their experiences.

This tolerance for failure or even celebration of failure is a defining characteristic of entrepreneurial hubs like Silicon Valley, and is an area in which, historically, many developing economies have not fared well. Rajesh Jain is one of India's early entrepreneurial success stories. He sold his company, Indiaworld, to Sify for ₹500 crore in 1999 at the beginning of the first wave of the Internet in India. He describes himself as a 'serial failure' and attributes his ultimate success to having multiple experiences of failure before finally tasting success. Jain is quick to admit that this attitude to failure was strengthened both by his background (he hails from a business family) and his professional exposure in the US at a formative age.

If you look at any group of graduate students from India in the 1980s, it is evident that the entrepreneurial orientation of students who went to the US to study engineering in the 1980s is much higher. Many of these students went abroad with a conservative, scholarly approach. A key difference was that in the US, having a failed start-up was something to be worn as a badge of honour. Slowly, a stress on entrepreneurship and incubation is beginning to take hold even in India, and a necessary condition for such an entrepreneurial culture is a change in a society's attitude to risk-taking and failure.

A well-rounded schooling system: A school system that encourages students to have multiple interests allows children to discover themselves as multi-faceted human beings. In the absence of this, education may tend to focus on some subjects and neglect the development of others. Learnability implies the nurturing of a well-rounded curiosity, and the biggest barrier to curiosity is an excessive emphasis on finding the single right answer. Girish Nair, an IIT-educated engineer turned entrepreneur, has founded a company called Curiosity Gym based out of Mumbai. Each gym is an environment where children can play with 3D printers, drones and other tools of creation. Curiosity Gym attempts to strengthen an attitude towards experimentation and play in the middle- and senior-school levels and has been adopted enthusiastically by many of Mumbai's top schools. The stress on questioning and curiosity, both within and outside the school system, is essential to building learnability and has hitherto been seen only in a few select Indian schools.

Diversity: Exposure to diversity (income, age, gender, occupation, race, religion, language, and so on) in day-to-day life helps an individual recognize very early on that their habits, beliefs and approach to life are not singular. When diversity and harmony flourish in the same environment, it usually leads to greater mental and emotional flexibility, an appreciation of alternative viewpoints and an inclusive mindset.

Learnability is the software that will drive the manager of tomorrow. It encompasses the beliefs, know-how and mindset that the ability to keep an individual relevant. Marilee Adams, a school teacher in the US and a highly successful educator, has written a book titled *Change Your Questions, Change Your Life*. The essential premise of the book is that most people, when they face failure or disappointment, are quick to adopt a judgemental mindset. Typically, this says 'the world is bad' or 'I am bad'.

In organizational environments, this means blaming the boss, the team or the organization at large. The converse is the learner mindset, which involves asking questions designed to understand the situation better and moving to purposive action. This could involve a shift from 'My boss does not listen' to 'What can I do differently to get through to my boss?' With many examples, she demonstrates the power of inculcating the learner mindset in school children.

Note that two individuals may both have a high degree of learnability, but may vastly differ in their ability to adapt quickly to the unfamiliar or unknown. Adaptability is the output of learnability, and the manager of tomorrow must be able to both learn and adapt.

Adaptability

Adaptability is defined in the *Oxford English Dictionary* as the 'ability to adjust quickly to new conditions'. While adaptability requires an individual to have the ability to learn, it also involves their ability to quickly sense and respond to a situation, which goes beyond learnability. Adaptability can thus have the following components:

Openness to your environment: This is the ability to receive feedback from both internal and external sources, and quickly gauge whether the current assumptions and styles of operation are misplaced. More flexible and less hierarchical organizations and leadership styles that involve regular contact with external and internal stakeholders help to foster this openness.

A bias for action: It is not enough to receive feedback openly. A recognition of urgency, a willingness and ability to reconsider patterns that have worked in the past and the ability to combine reflection and action are necessary for adaptability. Many organizations develop a pride in their own success and a set of assumptions that govern their way of working that are implicitly drawn from past success.

Joel Barker, author, film-maker and lecturer on paradigms,

talks about the story of the Swiss watch industry. Quartz watches were invented in Switzerland, but not adopted by the Swiss watch industry. Initially, the industry which prided itself on precision and mechanical craftsmanship, decried the quartz watch because it did not have movements. The concerned inventor took his idea to an international exhibition and it was adopted enthusiastically by Japanese watchmakers. The resulting innovation set the Swiss watch industry back by many years.

Similarly, the 'Statistical Product Quality Administration' was conceived by W. Edwards Deming in the US but initially received a cold reception from US auto companies. His ideas were adopted enthusiastically by Japanese car makers and his influence was at the heart of the subsequent Japanese dominance of the US automobile market. The implicit sense of arrogance and seeing something as 'not invented by us' is a barrier to new action and the human mind is quite ingenious in its ability to identify reasons why something should not be done.

The environmental factors that foster adaptability include:

Experience of discontinuous change: Intuitively, successfully adapting to a situation gives an individual the confidence to deal with many kinds of situations. In our own experience, children from military families, whose parents are frequently posted in different locations, are used to adapting to multiple locations. In job interviews, one frequently sees such students talk with great specificity about how moving across locations and schools has made them view change more openly and develop an ability to make new friends. Therefore, an exposure to changes in the course of one's life, as well as the daily habit of dealing with unpredictable conditions, helps us develop robust contingency planning mechanisms.

Scarcity: A constrained environment enables better use of resources. International students from affluent backgrounds are initially taken aback when they visited an impoverished area in an emerging economy. SPJIMR has a partnership with the Tata Group, whereby students from international universities are exposed to problems faced by the less privileged social sector in India. Their presentations suggest that the experience changes them profoundly, and, among other things, they realize that many families live in spaces that are smaller than their hostel rooms. Vodafone, the leading telecom multinational, exposes its leaders to a social sector challenge prior to taking over a business-head role.

Leaders report that the experience changes their orientation to resource management and the ability to get things done under severe constraints.

Language: While exposure to diversity fosters an individual's ability to learn and adapt to differences across people and contexts, the world of tomorrow's global organization involves communication and decision-making across geographical boundaries. English is the language of the global economy. Association to Advance Collegiate Schools of Business (AACSB), the world's pre-eminent accrediting body for management education and Graduation Management Admission Council (GMAC) both report a growth in the number of universities in Germany and China which are opening their doors to international education. This implies an increase in the options for post-graduate education in English in these countries. The ability to think and speak in English and to communicate with people with differing levels of language familiarity and comfort will be useful. Countries that have a stronger foundational schooling in the English language will have an advantage in the adaptability stakes.

Familiarity with technology: Early exposure to the latest technologies and a strong education system focusing on science and technology are both needed for individuals to embrace emerging technologies. Any initial disadvantage here is likely to grow as the pace of upgradation will only get faster.

Learnability and adaptability will, thus, be defining characteristics of tomorrow's successful managers. Of course, these are not the only characteristics, but they will, *ceteris paribus*, separate the best from the rest. While some of these aspects seem to work in favour of prospective managers from developing countries with a strong formative English language education, there are aspects which work in just the opposite direction. The upbringing of the Indian manager still places tremendous emphasis on financial security along with a stigma attached to failure and experimentation, and this often implies a tendency to look at safer options.

The made-in-India manager has, by virtue of his upbringing, built resilience and adaptability. In order to translate this to success in the larger world of organizations, the would-be manager needs to develop a balanced attitude to risk-taking, which implies an enhanced ability to understand his or her formative influences and adopt approaches that are tailored to both context and opportunity.

8 SELF-KNOWLEDGE

'You have to grow from the inside out.'

– Swami Vivekananda

IN 1955, AT A HUMAN RELATIONS CONFERENCE IN OJAI, CALIFORNIA, two senior researchers were asked to present their summary of the day's proceedings. While preparing this summary, Joseph Luft and Harrington Ingham, reputed psychologists at the University of California, Berkeley, came up with a simple 2x2 matrix to explain the quality of interpersonal relationships. At its core, the framework advocates openness to feedback and self-disclosure as the tools to expand the productive content of human relationships. The framework, which has come to be called the Johari window after its creators, has been adopted across the world to understand interpersonal relationships in the workplace.

The particular tenet of the Johari window that is relevant to our discussion is this – relevant self-disclosure and the willingness to seek, receive and act on feedback are necessary in order for managers to have high self-awareness. Self-awareness itself is a weaker form of Warren Bennis's tenets of self-knowledge and is a significant, but not sufficient, condition for learnability.

We Can Only Improve That Which We Understand

Warren Bennis puts it succinctly and states, 'Until you truly know yourself, strengths and weaknesses, know what you want to do and why you want to do it, you cannot succeed in any but the most superficial sense of the word.' He also goes on to say, 'You are your own raw material.' It is impossible for us to improve and come to terms with that which we do not understand in our own selves.

Increasingly, managers are required to adapt to a variety of people and situations. While adaptability to situations can be built by an exposure to ambiguity and diversity while growing up, adaptability to people requires the manager to understand both himself and the other. This premise is at the heart of self-awareness and is a defining characteristic of many successful leaders. We can make a fairly strong case here that for Indian managers of today, defined earlier as those who had their formative education in the late 1970s and 1980s, the ability to understand themselves and others around them was not something their upbringing prepared them for.

Restricted Awareness

Middle-class Indian education, both at school and at home, stressed the value of education and educational attainment. Typically, this translated to a strong focus on mathematics and science. The purpose of education was to prepare young people for lucrative and secure careers, and chartered accountancy, engineering and medicine were seen as the most desirable among the options available. Management studies was an option for postgraduate qualification, but at that point, for the ascendant middle class, studying for a master's degree abroad was as good (if not better) than doing a management degree at a premier Indian school. This led to an educational and social system that strongly emphasized success in the hard subjects, subjects that are typically perceived as being left-brained, that is, essentially, subjects related to logic, mathematics and systematic analysis.

If you had to compete in an intense academic environment, you had to be able to analyse your own performance and find ways to work systematically towards getting better. In itself, this led to an early exposure to self-awareness in domains of interest. The way to get better at subjects was to work hard and link approaches to results. Both within and outside the school system, Indian students had access to focused coaching which built quantitative skills and identified methods geared to help them succeed in competitive examinations. More than anything else, our education system told us that hard work, early identification and correction of errors, experimentation with alternative approaches and practise were the paths to achieving excellence in domains that mattered.

The limitation, of course, was that some domains mattered more than others. A student who scored well at both mathematics and English would inevitably be pushed towards the former. The system implicitly encouraged some skills more than others, and it would not be unfair to state that our system had a strong, implicit bias for IQ over EQ. If a student was interested in creative writing or debating, these were encouraged and were a source of pride. But these skills were an add-on to the student's main focus, the analytical subjects.

Low Focus on Social Skills

Arun Maira, the noted Indian thinker, recently advocated that the Indian education system needs to include listening skills in school and college curricula. The skills of listening, reflective conversation and being able to understand and work with different people have traditionally not been amongst the strengths of our education system. It has long been understood that while these are useful skills, they are nowhere near as critical as the fundamental ability to structure, analyse and solve problems. Hence, these skills, which may be innate in many people, lie under-explored and underdeveloped. Not only does this result in a relative weakness when it comes to social skills, but also an orientation towards analysis, which implies a strong focus on right answers, and a relative inability to link reason and emotion into a holistic view of a problem and its solution.

Satya Nadella sometimes cites the story of his first-ever interview at Microsoft. He was asked how he would react if he sees a small baby crying in the middle of the road. His response was that he would call 911. The response was rational and effective but, as the interviewer informed him, a little short on empathy. The first human response in this instance should be to pick up the baby, the interviewer suggested. In an interview with the *Wall Street Journal*, Bill Gates talked about Nadella having a 'natural way to work well with a lot of people'. In his own book, *Hit Refresh*, Nadella underscores the importance of empathy, patience and collaboration, and suggests that these are skills that he has built up over the years.

How can successful managers of Indian origin, whose social skills have often been systematically de-emphasized, manage to build self-awareness and develop these skills to the point where they can be considered a workplace advantage? Some answers may be found in the nature of the institutions that the made-in-India manager is exposed to in his formative years.

The Student Hostel as the Crucible of the World

Education up to the twelfth standard is followed by competitive examinations, which lead to undergraduate education at institutions like the IITs, regional engineering colleges, the All India Institute of Medical Sciences (AIIMS), and so on. Students compete for a spot on a national level and a large number have to leave their home towns to study at these institutes. For many, this is the initiation into staying away from home.

Staying in a hostel is a significant change for sheltered children. They are exposed to a large number of people who come from different locations, have different interests and speak different languages. The second shock comes from discovering that there are many students with higher abilities than them, and it is no longer easy to be the best in class. While this can be a cause of insecurity for some, most students tend to adjust and take it in their stride. Consequently, they learn to live and work with peers of comparable or higher ability or motivation. Undergraduate campuses often offer greater choices and opportunities in terms of recreation and extracurricular activities, and for many students this is a time and place to discover more holistic interests.

Hostels allow students to forge deep friendships at a formative age, discover and express interests outside academics and accept the fact that there are many competitions that they will not win, irrespective of ability and effort. A hostel also provides an environment that fosters an appreciation of collaboration and a sense of community. There are a large number of successful made-in-India managers who have come from a hostel environment and credit the people they met in a school or college hostel, and the experiences they had there, as instrumental in their future success.

It is also possible for the hostel experience to transform and open up hitherto unexplored talents. In some cases, it may cause a student to retreat into a group of similar people, individuals with talents in some dimensions, but whose insecurity stops them from stepping outside those dimensions successfully. The ability to leverage new experiences for holistic personal growth is dependent on the elusive construct of a mindset and it is useful to set some context of how and why it matters.

The Growth Mindset

Carol Dweck, the famed Stanford University psychiatrist, has developed and demonstrated that there are two mindsets that one can have towards ability. The first is what she calls a '***fixed mindset***', which holds that ability is largely innate and is the most important predictor of success. Conversely, she also posits and espouses a '***growth mindset***'. Here, the premise is that ability is like a muscle. It can be grown by stretching, determination and the willingness to experiment. Through a series of experiments, Dweck demonstrates that a growth mindset is required to build sustained success. Somebody with a growth mindset is far more likely to react to feedback positively and be willing to confront vulnerability. We have seen that Indian parenting and education systems reinforce the values of determination and practice as a route to excellence, and hence inculcate a growth mindset in academic domains.

Conversely, if a student fails despite strong effort and is berated indiscriminately, either by a parent or teacher, it leads to a lack of openness to failure and feedback and will engender a fixed mindset. Many people lose the ability to respond to feedback because they have received censure masquerading as feedback early on in their lives.

The distinction between feedback and censure is largely

one of intent. Censure often fails to distinguish between the individual and the behaviour, and projects the frustration or insecurity of the person who is criticizing. Feedback, on the other hand, is given out of concern and a desire to improve the other, and focuses on behaviour in a constructive way. Early and destructive criticism can result in the building of mental walls and insecurity, which then refuse to let feedback in. In his popular TED Talk on 'creative confidence', David Kelley underscores this when he speaks of the large number of people in his seminars who have had their confidence undermined by a critical evaluation from a parent, teacher or peer and the lack of openness that it fosters.

Sometimes, parenting and education also excessively emphasize certain abilities and interests over others. Quantitative abilities, analytical skills and the ability to correctly solve structured problems within the boundaries of a predefined framework are strongly valued. This focus also implies that many skills are unexplored and can make an individual feel under-confident. The student can also develop fairly fixed notions of what she or he can and cannot do. In our role as management educators, it is not uncommon to find students who come to us with problems such as 'I know I am not good at networking' or 'I'm not the networking type' or 'I want to do consulting, but I am not good at making presentations in public'. When questioned about where the individual has drawn this conclusion from, it often turns out to be based on a single incidence of perceived public failure or criticism from a significant authority figure in early childhood. Thus, it is not uncommon for Indian students to have a fixed mindset in social domains and a growth mindset in largely intellectual domains.

Clearly, having a fixed mindset in social domains cannot be an advantage as a manager. However, in such cases, some aspects of upbringing can come to the rescue of the manager-to-be.

Let us assume that these managers have had the experience of deep connection and inclusivity in the family domain and have experienced strong, enduring relationships. During their time in a hostel or at an early stage in their first jobs, they receive feedback that success in the social domain is critical to future success and that the lack of social skills has the potential to adversely impact their future prospects. The Indian managers who make it to the top respond to this by digging deep within themselves, understanding themselves better and consciously making an effort to 'open up'. Essentially, they are able to use the algorithm of focused hard work, process improvement, experimentation and practice to build new skills on the job. Not all Indian managers make this transition, but those who do can go on to become spectacularly successful.

One of our contemporaries started his career with one of India's most visible private corporations. He said that when he began, he had a strong notion of getting on with 'my type of people'. Being academically brilliant, this attitude had not affected him adversely as a student because he'd always found a group of like-minded people. Yet, six months into his first job, at the start of a long career in marketing, he was told that while his technical skills were of the highest order his social skills would be critical to his success and he had to 'become less of an introvert'.

His response to this news was counter-intuitive, but it worked. He went back to books, reading the popular works of authors like Dale Carnegie and Steven Covey, and tried to correlate their theories to the behaviour of the successful people he observed in the workplace. He then experimented with those behaviours from the theories that made sense to him. Surprisingly, the experiment changed him. He found out that a lot of information in business was soft information and could be obtained through social networks, and that people could actually be rather interesting when you approached them with an open mind.

Two years later, the same company lauded him for his people skills and gave him a promotion to a position that required a high degree of interpersonal communication. He went on to become a successful corporate leader who is known across the board for his ability to understand and inspire people. Describing his transformation, he says, 'I used to meet people and look for things that were not there. Today, I look for things that are there.'

Formative experiences play a big part in the ability to reach into yourself, and the willingness to see your capabilities as a work in progress is an important consequence.

The Importance of Inclusion

Anant J. Talaulicar, the former managing director of Cummins India, remembers that school lunches were something he always looked forward to as a child. 'There were children from many different states, religions and cultures at school, and we would always share our food.' The idea that differences can contribute to a richer experience was clearly seeded early for him. When Anant went abroad later and was the only Indian posted at a factory in the US, it was initially difficult for him to be well integrated with a group that was predominantly of American origin. However, childhood lessons in inclusivity helped him approach this experience with a sense of openness and comfort, and became a major contributor to his success and growth.

Much later, as a leader at Cummins India, Anant created the vision of 'a workforce that is representative of India'. In a manufacturing dominated sector, with the percentage of women in the workforce being in the single digits, Anant enabled a transformation of the company from a traditional one to one of India's most diverse organizations, with over 30 per cent women in the workforce, many of them working successfully on the shop floor. The inclusion policies at Cummins certainly had their roots in the lunchroom of a Mumbai school.

Inclusion and openness to diversity are inculcated early in India, both within and outside the family, and in a world striving hard for inclusion, this may stand the manager of tomorrow in good stead.

A Greater Self-Awareness?

The manager brought up in India in the 1970s and 1980s differs in many respects from the millennial manager of tomorrow. The millennial manager has grown up in a post-liberalization era. There are many things that are beginning to change in India but equally there are things that have not changed. The Indian education system continues to place a high emphasis on hard work. Entrance examinations to educational institutions have become more competitive as the gap in exposure and access between the metropolitan cities and smaller ones in India is narrowing. What has changed, however, is the variety of alternative careers available and the willingness to pursue them. Within the school system itself, there is a growing emphasis on activity-based learning, extracurricular and team pursuits, and a small but perceptible shift towards a better-rounded education.

However, some countervailing trends are cause for concern. Millennials of today spend a lot of time with screens and much of their human interaction happens through technology. There is a resultant push towards instant gratification and fewer intimate, personal friendships are formed. Within families, there is a positive trend towards both parents being in the workforce. However, an undesirable consequence of this may be a reduction in the physical time that parents and children spend together. Coupled with increased materialism, these trends may create a disturbing counterpoint – the manager who enters the workplace today may be more insecure and more disadvantaged than the previous generation in terms of the ability to cope with faliure and form deep connections. Today, across campuses, counselling and providing mental healthcare for young students seems to be a much stronger trend.

We have seen many young students who come to premier business schools and experience deep anxiety and isolation during their first few months there. This is a well-documented trend today across premier institutes all over the country.

The sudden realization that one cannot and will not always come out on top and the inability to share vulnerability with peers, coupled with a very strong outcome orientation, can be crippling for some. While there are many students who are able to come to grips with these changes, the presence of support networks and appropriate institutional guidance are critical to nurturing today's managers in their formative phases.

Whether the insecurities of the prospective manager will be resolved in a manner beneficial to them ultimately depends on the strengths of the value-based upbringing that the individual has grown up with and internalized. Self-confidence built by early success in some domains and lack of exposure in others can lead to an insecure façade of self-belief, which, at its worst, can lead to destructive hubris. There is a fine line dividing arrogance and self-confidence, and finding a sense of gratitude and humility is critical to staying on the right side of this line.

9 A LESSON IN HUMILITY

'You have to take ownership and leadership of tomorrow. For that to be possible, you have to strengthen your capacity and widen your vision as a global citizen.'

– Ban Ki-moon

SOMETIME IN THE 1950S, DON MERWIN, THE PRODUCER OF a radio show, visited Albert Einstein's home in Princeton, New Jersey, to record an episode. As the recording was being set up, Einstein started asking Merwin about the recording device and how it worked. Einstein was curious about the underlying electronics of the fairly new device. Merwin, an electronics enthusiast, launched into a detailed explanation. A short while later, he stopped mid-sentence because he realized that he was lecturing Albert Einstein on physics!

Albert Einstein is known to have been a remarkably humble man. The same is often said of the late Dr A.P.J. Abdul Kalam, erstwhile president of India and a renowned scientist, and the managing director of the Delhi Metro Rail Corporation, E. Sreedharan. These are people who are better known for their actions and contribution and less for the positions they have held.

The word 'humility' comes from the Latin word *humilitas*, which can be translated as 'grounded' or 'from the earth'. A quality that is described in many religious texts, all of which place it on a pedestal, humility has a number of aspects, including recognizing the abilities of others and recognizing one's own limitations

It is important to understand that humility lies in the gap between pride or arrogance and self-deprecation. Humility and self-confidence are consistent and not contradictory. Why is humility so important for the global manager? Because managers of tomorrow will face an environment that is rapidly changing on multiple fronts. In order to manage in a VUCA world, the manager needs to recognize that the same qualities and approaches that were at the foundation of yesterday's success could be the cause of failure in the future. This implies that the ability to understand current assumptions, examine current reality with openness, and unlearn and relearn rapidly are critical to success tomorrow – more so than knowledge and past track record.

However, it is in the nature of human beings to take credit for their successes, and to project all or some aspects of their failure on factors beyond their control. How, then, do managers acquire humility?

Gratitude and Simplicity

If we consider the Indian manager, some seeds of humility are sown into them within the family structure. As children growing up in middle-class India, we are constantly reminded that there are many who are less fortunate than we are and that we should be grateful for what we have. Acknowledging the element of chance in our current status, and regularly being exposed to the concept of thanking a higher being for what we have been blessed with can seed early foundations of humility.

This consideration for the less fortunate and a direct exposure to economic struggle within our own families emphasizes simplicity in all aspects of life and creates an aversion to excessive ostentation. While it could be argued that the tendency for simple living varies dramatically across different regions in the country, many of us have seen, both by observed example and by actual storytelling, that being immodest and flashy carries implications of being insensitive to the struggles of others.

Humility and Adaptability

As we have seen, competitive intensity is very high in the Indian system, and most students must come to grips with the realization that success at an early academic stage is no guarantee of success at the next stage. The idea that success is not strictly in one's control and the recognition of superior ability in others is an important building block of humility.

Humility can also be forged early on by the realization that many things in the external environment cannot be relied upon to be consistent. An acceptance of uncertainty and ambiguity helps to reduce the illusion of control and create adaptability. The following anecdote from the early childhood of one of the authors (Ranjan) illustrates this.

'We grew up knowing that many aspects of life were unpredictable. I was five years old when the India–Pakistan war [of 1965] happened and was living in Mumbai. I have vague recollections of the blackout. The lights would go out and we would all have to be very silent and still. A little while later, a siren would go off and then it would be fine to put the lights on and things would go back to normal.

'Every summer, we would visit my grandmother's house in Adra in rural West Bengal. This was a completely different experience for us. There were mango and lemon trees everywhere. We learned how to climb up a tree and suck the pulp out of a mango without plucking it from the tree. We also learned that electricity was not something to be taken for granted. It was not uncommon for there to be no electricity for six to seven hours every day. But life would simply go on. Multiple kerosene lanterns would be lit, and if you wanted to read, you read. If you did not, there were hand fans and a fire to sit around. It was important, this unpredictability. We learned implicitly that systems did not always work and when that happened you had to have a plan B. Sometimes, you had to create that plan B at short notice from current resources. We learned this early and on multiple occasions.'

For many Indian managers, humility is deeply inculcated throughout their upbringing and these lessons are reinforced by an early initiation in professional Indian organizations. Many companies like Asian Paints, Unilever, Citibank, the Tata Group and Cadbury pride themselves on their ability to select talent with a strong educational background and grounded upbringing, and then equip them with an orientation that helps them transit from 'campus to corporate'. An important way to achieve this is through the curated learning experience.

The Curated Learning Experience

Let us take a close look at the initiation practices at HUL in India. On joining, HUL gives each management trainee a contact book. Each time a trainee meets a senior manager and has an interaction across a table, the contact book is offered to the senior manager to share his impressions of the trainee in writing. Potentially unnerving for a raw trainee straight out of business school, this gives a manager-to-be an early exposure to constructive feedback and enhances their ability to make use of such feedback.

At the end of six months, management trainees at Asian Paints are asked to make a presentation on an aspect of company operations to a senior management team – usually the first-line leadership of the organization. The presentation is meant to be stressful and trainees are asked challenging questions about their ideas and vision. These experiences are specifically designed to build resilience and humility and to equip prospective managers with the kind of self-confidence that is quiet and tempered by the experience of bouncing back from failure.

At SPJIMR, we have tried to build some of these ideas into the MBA curriculum. All students of our flagship two-year MBA course are part of a unique programme called Abhyudaya, in which they mentor school-going children from underprivileged areas near the school. The programme also involves a fortnightly visit to the child's home. Being a part of Abhyudaya enables MBA students, who are often from fairly affluent families, to see the world through the eyes of a different other, and many have described the experience as humbling or life-changing.

In a number of cases, students stay in touch with their mentees years after the formal course has ended. In the words of one of the coordinators of Abhyudaya, 'When students come to us, they usually complain about the size of their room in the hostel. However, when they visit the mentee's homes, they quickly realize that four people are living in a room smaller than theirs. Often, students admit that they learn more from their mentees than the mentees learn from them.'

While many aspects of how Indian managers are groomed point to a case for lessons in humility, there are factors that suggest that there is more to how managers can be humble than evident at the surface. India is a hierarchical society, and positions and the trappings around these positions are important to people. It is not unusual to see large contingents of people present at an airport or a railway station to receive senior leaders of parties or an organization. The rituals of garlanding and the touching of feet or other gestures communicating respect are common.

Hierarchy in India is signalled in many different ways – from the allotment of larger offices and elevated designations to even separate toilets and eating facilities for senior managers. This kind of culture is often not conducive to the building and growth of humility. Warren Bennis, in his writings, places a great deal of emphasis on wanting to *do* leadership as opposed to wanting to *be* leadership. However, often, positional power becomes an aspiration in itself due to the rewards associated with it. Leadership positions in different walks of life come with status and privilege. This is not only restricted to significantly higher monetary rewards and the trappings of a larger house, car and more, but also implies exposure and inclusion in a different social circle.

The best leaders are able to go beyond this by staying focused on leadership as an opportunity to contribute. Clayton M. Christensen, a well-known Harvard professor and one of the world's top experts on innovation and growth, talks about the social contribution that managers make in his book *How Will You Measure Your Life?: Finding Fulfilment Using Lessons from Some of the World's Greatest Businesses.* He explains that if employees feel validated and empowered at work, it impacts their self-esteem and energy, the way they interact with their family and children, and leads to a happier and more complete family life. In this sense, managers can see themselves as having the potential to positively impact the lives of employees who work with them. Where this is not true, positional power can lead to arrogance, isolation from reality and an ultimate fall from grace. Many such cases exist, from Kenneth Lay to Vijay Mallya, and are well documented.

The stress on competition and high selectivity often leads to students from India's best institutions to perceive themselves as being 'the chosen ones'. There is increasing talk amongst industry watchers and leaders about the sense of entitlement that our best and brightest seem to carry. It is important for prospective managers to realize that education gives them the foundation to succeed in an industry, but a significant part of the journey begins when they actually join a company and start learning through doing.

Prasanta Choudhury, the former managing director of VIP Industries and the man at the helm when the famous '*kal bhi, aaj bhi*' advertising campaign was created for the brand, had a unique way of addressing this issue. After management graduates had finished their initial orientation at VIP, they were brought to a room for a brief address from the CEO. The message was short but effective: 'Your MBA has brought you into this room. Congratulations.' He paused a moment and then said, 'You're on your own now.'

The Core of Learnability

Today, humility is more important than ever before because it is the single attribute at the core of learnability. In a study on lifelong learning published in 1982, learning theorists

Donald Mocker and George Spear tell us that there are three types of learning:

Formal learning: This happens via classrooms, formal orientation programmes, and executive development programmes within companies.

Informal learning: This happens through peer interactions and mentoring and is often a consequence of the socialization that accompanies formal learning.

Self-directed learning: This happens when individuals reflect on their own experiences or assess their own capabilities relative to what the world will need tomorrow. Then, either through reading or conscious experimentation, they plan and execute their plans to learn and build capabilities for the future.

It is estimated that more than 80 per cent of learning in the future will be driven by self-directed learning. This implies that taking responsibility for one's own learning is increasingly critical to sustained success.

Lifelong Learning and the Manager of Tomorrow

On the whole, there is enough reason to suggest that managers of tomorrow will be better equipped than managers of previous generations to be lifelong learners. The reason is their digital awareness. Today's generation of managers are digital natives. Often, they have learned subjects that interest them through the Internet well before they have entered a formal classroom. The classroom and the textbook are no longer the primary source of learning.

The Internet has also led to the democratization of access, and this means that tomorrow's managers have often pursued multiple interests on their own. When our children find that a teacher is unable to give them the clarity that they are looking for, they quickly move to the Internet and use various sources to understand the topic. The education system in India is beginning to evolve and is now more open to participative, activity-oriented learning within the school system. International school curricula like the International Baccalaureate and the IGCSE are more focused on questioning knowledge and discussion.

Academia now also allows for the simultaneous pursuit of multiple interests – from learning music independently to learning yoga. In parallel, world-class institutions are coming up in areas like law, liberal arts, fashion, design and other specialized fields of study, and providing students with the benefits of high-quality education in multiple streams.

However, there are certain limiting trends that also need to be acknowledged. Tomorrow's managers expect to be led in a far less hierarchical way. They want to have a say in their own future and are less likely to follow instructions blindly. We have frequently met managers who complain about a new manager's 'lack of discipline' and lack of respect for 'company culture'. Younger managers, on the other hand, are quick to complain about bosses whose 'attitudes are stuck in the past'. Often, if you ask the same senior managers how their own children are likely to behave in the workplace, they begin to see that what they are dealing with is not an attitude problem but rather a generational shift in attitudes to hierarchy and collaboration. It could also be argued that new managers have not had to deal with economic struggle and have multiple career options. This, in turn, may lead to a lower willingness to adapt and a fight-or-flight reaction in the face of workplace adaptability.

We live in a more narcissistic world today. Tata Consultancy Services (TCS), one of India's most successful technology companies, recently held a national conclave where it discussed adapting products to the 'selfie consumer'. This is a sign of the times. We also live in an evolving world, a world where friendships and achievements are instantly shared, where relationships break up over a text message, where high levels of self-expression are the rule, where conversations come with a word limit, where shopping can happen in four clicks of a mouse – and all of these point to instant gratification as the norm. This does not augur well for the qualities of patience and resilience and many point to the disturbing rise in the sense of entitlement of prospective managers, which seems to be increasing with every generation.

There are, however, two sides to every coin. Our overall contention is that the emerging characteristics of the millennial manager, if well harnessed, can lead to a more energetic, open and collaborative environment, where young managers get early responsibility and quickly make their presence felt. In that environment, the strengths of the millennial come to the fore, and we are able to leverage both similarities and differences in enabling the manager of tomorrow.

We believe that the world is ready for a new generation of Indian managers – ones who have seen India succeed on a global stage and possess a deeper self-confidence. They combine this with technology readiness, a hunger to compete on the global stage and the grounded resilience and adaptability that comes from having learned many things the hard way. There is no guarantee that this will lead to success, but we are confident that under a set of likely conditions, it is quite feasible to expect that this can be the shape of things to come.

CONCLUSION

IT IS FAIRLY EVIDENT TODAY THAT THE OCEAN OF BUSINESS management is influenced by two strong currents – first, the evolution of modern management thinking and, second, the multicultural fabric of lessons emerging from the task of managing structured organizations spread across the world.

As operating managers in an international environment, we have observed very many approaches. In particular, the modern Indian manager represents a unique confluence of Western and Eastern schools of management. There are a number of similarities and differences between these schools and practices of management, and it is worth reiterating some of the important ones to round up our argument.

Dealing with Ambiguity

Due to the influence of rationalists, Western management thinking abhors ambiguity. A manager must be adept at quickly sorting out issues, and the zone of ambiguity must be minimized. Indians accept ambiguity as an inevitable fact of life. One can try to reduce it, but a manager's real skill lies in managing the ambiguous. For example, in multinational corporations, job descriptions, reporting lines and organograms are quite often written in stone. In many Indian companies, these are loose and flexible, and it is actually seen as beneficial to keep them that way.

Decision-making

In multinational corporations, decision-making and conflict resolution follow a straight line. With the idea of empowerment gaining much ground, these organizations try very hard to delegate by explicit specification of authority schedules and aggressive goal-setting. If decisions are held up due to conflicting viewpoints, the issue is expected to speedily traverse up the line for a resolution. In the Indian context, two possibilities exist. Sometimes, there is no empowerment and, thus, many decisions are taken by the owner or the senior-most executive, achieving speed. Or, there is a form of delegation which requires consensus to be built, thus sacrificing speed and at times even motion itself! The inter-ministerial form of consultation practised in government is the best example of this.

Leadership

Western companies largely practice leadership by system. They institutionalize succession planning though their systems, admittedly with varying levels of efficiency. They like their managers to be valuable and skilled cogs in a well-oiled wheel of systems (information, budgets and reviews). If a manager at the top of the hierarchy changes, he or she would be missed but only temporarily until the new cog is operational. As an aside, the word 'cog' is misleading because it suggests little or no value addition by the manager; this is not an intended insinuation. It arises inevitably out of the machine metaphor.

In the Indian milieu, leadership is by personality. It is the magnetism and personal charisma of the manager at the top that is believed to make the difference. The systems surrounding this manager are not considered that important, though systems are perceived to have some value.

Status

Professor Fons Trompenaars points out in his book mentioned earlier that many Anglo-Saxons believe that ascribing status in an organization for reasons other than achievement is archaic and inappropriate to business. The

Indian mind accords status not purely by achievement but also by age, class, education and other parameters – it is an ascribed status.

Trompenaars quotes the example of a Swedish manager who had to make a choice between two Indian managers, both excellent for the job. He did his best to be objective and chose Mr A. Mr B was very upset and the Swedish manager found, to his great surprise, that what really rankled in Mr B's mind was that he had been senior in college to Mr A by two years. It made no sense to him to be passed over for a junior. One of the authors (Gopal) has observed such fixations with ascribed status in several cases during his own career. It is precisely this fixation that leads to a proliferation of bewildering designations – manager, senior manager, assistant general manager, deputy general manager, senior deputy general manager, and so on.

Doing Things

In Western companies, there is a great deal of emphasis on getting things done by analysis, logic and intellect – this, sometimes to a fault. There is a constant drive to get the most important facts and analysis on the table to take the right decision among many alternatives. In Indian companies, there is a desire to have more facts, but the means of obtaining these facts is often found lacking because a system that would efficiently do so has not been institutionalized. Partly because facts are not always available and partly, in Asia we believe, for various cultural reasons, things get done subjectively, intuitively and through connections. The systems of *guanxi* (building personal social networks of influence that facilitate the generation of new business) in China and *wasta* (utilizing connections and influence to things done) in Saudi Arabia are examples of this.

Openness

Being frank and open is a strong, important feature of Western companies. The Dutch culture takes this honesty to an extreme – if you ask a Dutch audience for criticism after a speech, the experience can be described as the closest to being machine-gunned! But in India being openly critical is not always considered a virtue. It is more important to be nice about one's opinion. 'If you shoot an arrow of truth, dip its point in honey,' says an Arab proverb, and this is true in India too. Perhaps this is the reason why Indians are thought to speak with forked tongues by some Westerners – most unfairly, of course!

The Indian Paradigm

In stating these differences, we have taken a certain amount of license with two things. First, with some generalizations about Western and Indian positions and, second, with some caricaturing as two polar opposites. We plead guilty to being a little simplistic but this has been done to allude to tendencies rather than stereotypes. We must also state that we do not have a judgement on right and wrong. We only seek to share a few perspectives based on our experience of working with many nationalities. The important thing is that there has to be, and will be, some convergence over time, but not congruence. The convergence will occur by certain Easternization of Western behaviour and some westernization of Eastern behaviour.

Westerners are often surprised that Easterners don't implement remedies and actions that are so obvious to them. Many Westerners, both in India and overseas, marvel at Indians, whose minds they find fascinating. Indians know perfectly well what is required to be done for their company to prosper, or even for their country to progress. Our clarity is stunning, our articulation of ideas is gripping. Where we fail is in doing what we know must be done.

A Country in Flux

Nobel Prize-winner Douglas North has explained that countries that emulate best practices from other nations are not always successful because those best practices do not necessarily match the heritage and values of the countries. We postulate that in India there is a cultural transformation at play – the fitting of a Western intellectual tradition to an Indian social context. We are not clear if or how a programme can be devised to accelerate this synthesis. It must happen naturally. We may not see this change in our lifetimes, but our experience and interpretation of the present leaves us optimistic.

However, an important question still begs an answer: Is there a way to ensure that the made-in-India manager will succeed globally in the coming decades? The answer is that given what the past has shown us and our observations of the trajectory of Indian management thought leadership and practice, the road ahead is indeed encouraging.

The Road Ahead: Suggestions for the Manager-to-Be

It does not, of course, stand to reason that the Indian manager, merely by virtue of origin and upbringing, is bound to succeed in a global environment. To tomorrow's manager and today's middle manager, we offer a few simple suggestions from experience.

Longevity Matters

It has been said by many that the millennial manager has grown up in a culture of instant gratification and is far less patient than today's manager. This impatience can be harnessed positively as a 'bias for action' and an ability to bring energy to a work environment. However, this bias for action can sometimes also mean premature rejection of a difficult boss or senior colleague, and the tendency to jump ship too quickly when confronted with a lack of expected autonomy. Learning within an organization takes time, as does the building of credibility. Often, the people who make it to the top within a group of talented managers and would-be leaders, are distinguished by many things. Among them staying power is an important component of that list.

Earning Your Right to Balance

A manager new to an organization has an expectation of work–life balance which is often quite different to those of senior leaders in the organization. Organizational rhetoric has changed and workplaces will evolve over time, but a new manager cannot, and should not, demand balance in the workplace from day one. Performance builds credibility, and with credibility comes the ability to foster a work culture where output is valued more than apparent long hours. New managers must have the patience and foresight to earn their right to balance. Change happens slowly, and each new manager, both by personal action and the way they treat their team, can help to make this transition happen smoothly.

Handling Success

There are many trappings of managerial success. For someone brought up in a middle-class environment, there is transition to a high level of material comfort and status. There is often adulation, media visibility and a certain degree of sycophancy that surrounds people in top positions. In many cases, this can lead to an inflated ego and could adversely impact the manager in two ways:

An obsession with material success: This is manifested in extravagant lifestyles, a tendency to flaunt material possessions and indulging in constant comparison with others. It results in insecurity and an inability to be comfortable with oneself.

An exaggerated sense of self-importance and narcissism: It is human nature to credit victories to oneself and failures to one's environment. Combined with the absence of feedback and a highly centralized working style, it can lead to a great deal of hubris. Examples of much-touted success stories of people who have had a spectacular fall from grace abound, and Indian managers have been no exception to this.

There are tools that can help to handle these dangers and they can be found in the roots of the Indian manager. Some of these are listed below:

Staying Connected to Your Core Values

The role of the family and the mentor are powerful. Indians overseas are quite diligent at keeping in touch with the family, and parental values of humility and respect help keep the manager grounded. Our experiences with today's students suggest that they belong to a generation that is more socially aware, one that is far more willing to get involved in causes beyond one's own success, and this can only help to develop humility in the face of success.

Mentoring is also a significant and long-standing Indian tradition, and the manager who stays in touch with leaders and role models he admires at the transition points in his life is likely to stay humbler. As teachers, we often get calls from former students when they are contemplating a career move, and there are many cases where we have seen our advice lead to productive and successful careers. Asking for help does not come easily to everyone, and the ability to reach out and cultivate mentors will serve tomorrow's manager well.

Quiet Confidence

This is perhaps the most important and final transition. One of the consequences of our colonial heritage (and, to a certain extent, visible material contrast), is that we have come to view ideas and products created in the West as being intrinsically superior to anything created in India. Would-be managers of tomorrow are not immune to this mindset, and the ability to express ideas confidently in an international forum when exposed for the first time needs to be cultivated. We are conscious of our accent, our nationality, the colour of our skin and our history. However, tomorrow's managers have travelled internationally at a much earlier age. They have seen more, done more and been exposed to more international role models of Indian origin. Under the right circumstances, this can translate to a quiet confidence, a confidence that does not need to constantly and loudly self-promote. This kind of manager has a deep focus on the job to be done, and faith in his or her ability to learn and master both the present and the uncertain future.

■

For all the reasons already discussed in this book, the influence of the made-in-India manager has been growing over the last half century. At the beginning of the book we had introduced the idea of emergence, which refers to the property of a system that results from a combination of particular elements of that system, a unique one that may not be exhibited by any of its constituent elements. For example, the beauty of a flower emerges from the arrangement of the petals within the flower – the beauty is not a property of the individual petal but a property of the system of petals that constitute the flower. Crucially, each petal is necessary to complete the design, and a missing petal may prevent the emergence of the flower's beauty.

As much as it is in the nature of a flower and its petals, there is a strong likelihood that in the years to come we will see the emergence of the factors we have discussed in this book in the Indian manager and in Indian management thought and practice.

Our perspectives on why the made-in-India manager has achieved such a great degree of global success and is positioned to achieve more may not strike a chord with every reader in every respect, but at the very least we hope that the subject will attract further study and scrutiny, deliberation and discussion. This book does not offer a definitive future prediction; it offers a sense of possibility. If this book is read and internalized by many, there is the happy prospect of the ideas in this book becoming a self-fulfilling prophecy. Nothing would please us more.

ACKNOWLEDGEMENTS

We have so many people to thank – their help and assistance in conceptualizing and writing this book has been invaluable. We will try to acknowledge them all, though we fear that we may miss some, for which our apologies in advance.

Firstly, our thanks to Poulomi Chatterjee of Hachette India. She brought this book to the fore from the thicket of ideas lurking in our minds. A special word for the Hachette editorial team and Niyati Dhuldhoya is called for. As authors, we wrote the original manuscript with a certain brief and purpose. As we progressed and delivered the first draft, the team saw a much bigger possibility from the book. They redesigned the brief and purpose, thus bombarding us with queries and suggestions. It was indeed exasperating on occasion, but we think we have a better book for it. We are also grateful to Semy Haitenlo, who designed the cover.

Second, we wish to thank all the young people who have fired our minds with their thoughts and inputs, the students at the S.P. Jain Institute of Management and Research, Mumbai. We have, along with Professor Jagdish Rattanani, engaged with over 300 students through an immersive programme called QYDNAS (Questions You Did Not Ask at SPJIMR). The freshness of their insights and questions greatly helped us to imagine the future while retaining our connections to the past.

We also thank the voices of experience, the made-in-India managers we know: Anant Talaulicar, chairman of Cummins India; P.K. Basu, a distinguished economist in Singapore; K.K. Sridhar, formerly at S.C. Johnson in Chicago; K.C. Ashok, who now advises start-ups and entrepreneurship companies in Boston; K.V. Rao, Tata Sons' resident director in Singapore; S.N. Venkat, adjunct professor at the Singapore Management University; and Phanish Puranam, professor at INSEAD, Singapore.

We are also grateful to the people who reviewed our manuscript: Nihal Kaviratne, former chairman of Unilever Indonesia; K. Jayakumar, managing director of Akzo Nobel India Ltd; B.K. Narayan, software professional in Washington DC; Professor Jagdish Rattanani of SPJIMR; and two long-serving professional managers, R. Narayanan and R. Srinivasan in Chennai. The strengths of our book most likely are inspired by their comments, and the weaknesses are entirely ours.

The authors would also like to thank each other. Writing a book together requires very different skills from writing alone. It has been a Ganga–Jamuna of thought processes, writing styles and literary skills. Much like the *sangam* in Allahabad, this book is a *sangam* of ourselves, sometimes showing indistinguishable mingling of the waters and sometimes showing two different streams coming together. We have taught each other a lot in the process.

Finally, to our wives, Geeta Gopalakrishnan and Anindita Banerjee – thank you for putting up so patiently with our odd timings.

R. Gopalakrishnan and *Ranjan Banerjee*
30 September 2018
Mumbai